A Resource Book
for Good Mental Health

NEW EDITION
1.3 MILLION COPIES IN PRINT

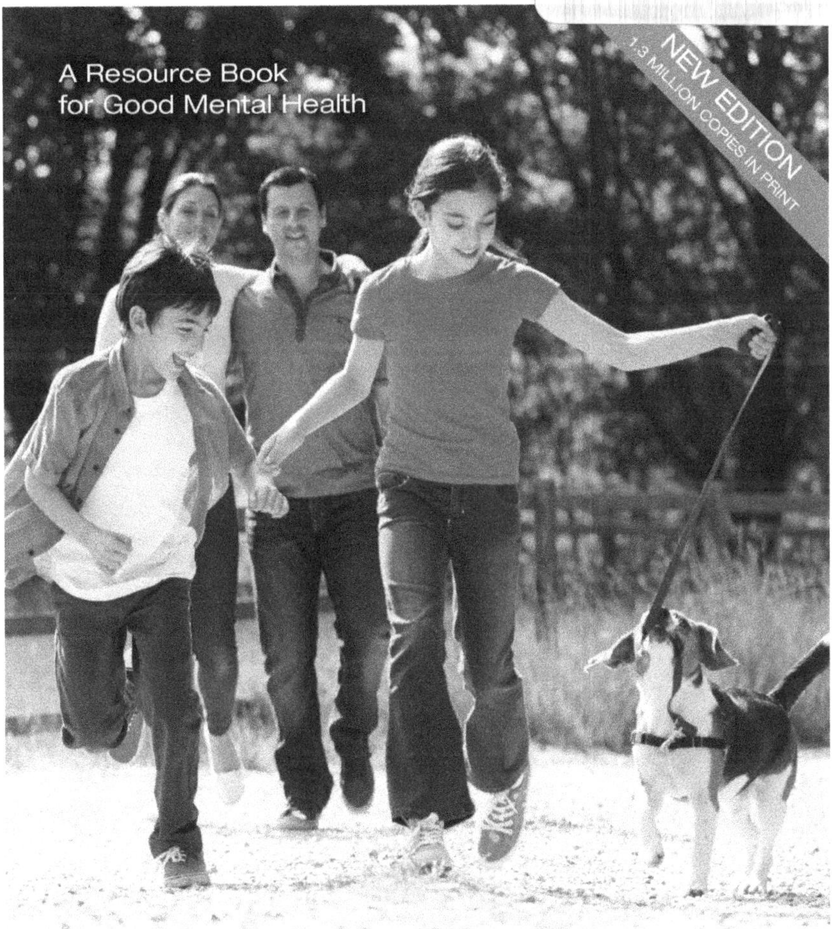

Taking Care of Yourself and Your Family

John Ashfield PhD

Taking Care
of Yourself and Your Family

A Resource Book for Good Mental Health

John Ashfield PhD

Published by You Can Help Publishing

Copyright © John Ashfield 2018

National Library of Australia Card Number & ISBN 978-0-9944664-4-0

Printed in Australia

All responsibility for editorial matters rests with the author(s). Any views or opinions expressed or advice given are therefore not necessarily those of **YouCanHelp Publishing**. The information and/or self-help resources in this publication are not intended as a substitute for mental health assessment, medical or psychiatric consultation, assessment or treatment.

No part of this document can be reproduced in any way without permission of **YouCanHelp** whose materials are protected under law with a registered trademark.
Permission can be sought from:
info@youcanhelp.com.au

CONTENTS

Introduction 7
Depression 9
Anxiety 45
Disturbing Thoughts 83
Insomnia 97
Conflict 123
Anger 131
Stress 145
Relationship Violence 177
Alcohol 185
Substances and Mental Health 207
Grief 211
Key Services and Resources 245
Helplines 239
    Aboriginal and Torres Strait Islander Services 242
    National Websites 243
Sources used in the preparation of this book 246

INTRODUCTION

Initially, this book was compiled for use by people in rural and remote areas of Australia who have little or no useful access to the kinds of counselling and psychotherapy support that people in urban centres can generally take for granted. While the book targets rural and remote Australians, it's also helpful for other people as well. Some people may be unable to access local mental health services due to the location and cost of these services, or due to work commitments and a lack of time. This book provides useful information and practical strategies to help promote good mental health for everyone.

Given the vast area of rural Australia, and the limited resources of community mental health services, it has proven difficult to focus effectively on measures of preventative mental health, as well as responding to the demands of mental health crises and people with longstanding mental health difficulties.

General medical practitioners are often frustrated in responding to the mental health needs of their patients, because they sometimes have little choice but to prescribe medication to control symptoms for which they would prefer to recommend psychological therapy, if it were available. Likewise, where a combination of medication and psychological therapy is needed, the former is often all that can be provided.

This book is not intended as a substitute for psychological therapy (or psychotherapy), or formal mental health assessment. But it does aim to provide an additional resource for prevention, early detection, intervention, self-help, and education in relation to some common mental health issues and mental health difficulties. Its design takes account of the known resourcefulness, self-reliance and resilience of many people who live in our often harsh and isolating rural and remote areas.

The topics covered in the book were chosen because they have been found to be the most recurrent themes encountered by doctors and other human service providers.

The intended uses of the book include:

- A source of basic information about a range of mental health and related issues.
- A guide for helping others, or prompting them to seek assistance, in the event of a mental health issue.
- A resource of strategies and self-help therapies that have been adapted from some widely used and documented standard psychological therapies.
- A resource that can be photocopied and self-help therapies that doctors can use as handouts for their patients.
- A resource for use in *basic* community mental health education.
- A resource for health and human service workers.

The content of the book is organised so that readers are not required to read any more information than they need or interests them. Problem identification checklists are placed at the beginning of relevant sections so that, even if no other part of the section is read, the checklist may be.

A number of the self-help resources (such as Structured Problem-Solving) are provided in more than one section, to avoid readers having to refer to another part of the book in addition to the section they are reading.

Language, practical examples, and some of the diagrams used have been selected in order to be gender inclusive, or 'user friendly' for men as well as women.

It is hoped that the information and resources of this book will not only stimulate interest and concern about mental health issues, but will contribute something to the capacity of Australians to take care of their own and each other's mental health – often despite limited professional services and support.

Depression

DEPRESSION CHECK

For more than **Two Weeks** have you: Tick if Yes

1. Felt sad, down or miserable most of the time? ○
2. Lost interest or pleasure in most of your usual activities? ○

If you answered 'Yes' to either of these questions, complete the symptom checklist below. If you did not answer 'Yes' to either of these questions, it is unlikely that you have a problem with depression.

3. Lost or gained a lot of weight?
   OR Had a decrease or increase in appetite? ○
4. Sleep disturbance? ○
5. Felt slowed down, restless or excessively busy? ○
6. Felt tired or had no energy? ○
7. Felt worthless? OR Felt excessively guilty?
   OR Felt guilt about things you should not have been feeling guilty about? ○
8. Had poor concentration? OR Had difficulties thinking?
   OR Were very indecisive? ○
9. Had recurrent thoughts of death? ○

Add up the number of ticks for your total score: ....

What does your score mean?

(assuming you answered 'Yes' to question 1 and/or question 2.)

4 or less: Unlikely to have depression
5 or more: Likely to have depression

If you have some of these symptoms and they are affecting your life:

TAKE ACTION
Arrange to speak to a doctor

Thoughts about suicide or self harm are serious.
If you are having these thoughts –

TAKE URGENT ACTION
Arrange to speak to a doctor OR phone

PHONE A 24-HOUR MENTAL HEALTH EMERGENCY LINE NATIONAL

Lifeline: 13 11 14
Suicide Call Back Service: 1300 659 467

State and Territory

- **ACT:** Crisis Assessment and Treatment Team: 1800 629 354
- **NSW:** Salvo Suicide Prevention & Crisis Line:
  Metro 02 9331 2000
  Salvo Suicide Prevention & Crisis Line:
  Rural 1300 363 622
  Suicide Prevention and Support: 1300 133 911
  NSW Mental Health Line: 1800 011 511
- **NT:** Mental Health on Call Team: Top End (08) 8999 4988
  Mental Health on Call Team: Central Australia
  (08) 8951 7710
- **QLD:** Salvo Crisis Counselling Service: Metro 07 3831 9016
  Salvo Crisis Counselling Service: Rural 1300 363 622
- **SA:** Mental Health Assessment and Crisis
  Intervention Service: 13 14 65
- **TAS:** Mental Health Services Helpline: 1800 332 388
- **VIC:** Mental Health Advice Line: 1300 280 737
  SuicideLine: 1300 651 251
- **WA:** Mental Health Emergency Response Line:
  Metro 1300 555 788
  Rural Link: Rural 1800 552 002
  Samaritans Crisis Line: 1800 198 313

National Help/Information Lines

Lifeline: 13 11 14
Kids Helpline: 1800 55 1800
Australian Psychological Society Referral Line: 1800 333 497
SANE Australia: 1800 18 7263
Relationships Australia: 1300 364 277

ABOUT DEPRESSION

Depression is more than just a low mood – it can be a serious condition. While we all feel sad, moody or low from time to time, some people experience these feelings intensely, for long periods of time and often without reason. People with depression find it hard to function every day and may be reluctant to participate in activities they once enjoyed.

Depression is one of the most common mental health problems. Over one million people in Australia experience depression each year.

Everyone has a bad day now and then. There is no shortage of life events that can leave us feeling distressed, disappointed or just plain lousy. The problem is when these kinds of feelings persist; when long-lasting changes in mood, feelings and behaviours develop into depression. And yet, on occasions, depression just seems to come out of nowhere, at a time when everything appears to be fine.

Many factors may contribute to depression including:

- **a family history** of depression
- **hormonal changes** (in women and men)
- **emotional stress** (e.g. bereavement, job loss, relationship breakdown)
- **medicines** (e.g. some cancer and heart medicines)
- **medical conditions** – such as thyroid and other hormone problems, or battling a chronic or terminal illness.
- **personality** – the type of person you are and how you respond to life events
- **social support** – whether you have sufficient supportive people around you. People isolated on farms or station properties may lack important social support.
- **life changes** – major life events such as the birth of a baby may increase the risk of developing depression.

What if depression is left untreated?

Getting the right therapy or treatment early is crucial to a person's recovery from depression. Left untreated, an episode of major depression may last from six to twelve months or longer. Half the people who recover from an untreated episode of depression will slip back into their former state of depression within two years of their first episode.

Depression can be a serious condition. Even 'minor' depression can become very disruptive to people's lives – more so than many physical disorders. However, when depression is properly treated, most people can expect a full recovery.

What are the treatments for depression?

Different types of depression require different types of treatment. This may include physical exercise for preventing and treating mild depression, through to psychological and drug treatments for more severe levels of depression. The major types of treatment for depression include psychological treatments, antidepressant medication, and self-help strategies.

> ### IMPORTANT
> - Self-help measures are no substitute for medication if medication is needed.
> - Thoughts about self-harm or suicide are serious. Speak to a doctor or call a 24 hour mental health crisis line immediately.

Psychological therapies

Psychological therapies deal with problems that particularly affect people with depression. These therapies help people to change negative patterns of thinking and/or sort out relationship difficulties.

Psychological therapies can help to:
- change negative thoughts and feelings
- encourage the person to get involved in activities
- speed the person's recovery
- prevent depression from recurring
- identify ways to manage depression and stay well.

One of the most commonly used psychological therapies is **Cognitive Behaviour Therapy** (CBT). This therapy teaches people to think realistically about common difficulties, helping them to change their thought patterns and the way they react to certain situations.

Interpersonal Therapy (IPT) is another psychological therapy which is used with people experiencing depression. It helps people find new ways to get along with others and to resolve losses, changes and conflict in relationships.

Psychological therapies may be provided by a number of health professionals (if the use of these therapies has been part of their training), including: GPs, psychologists, social workers, occupational therapists in mental health, and psychiatrists.

The self-help strategies provided in this chapter are based on psychological therapies.

If a person is only mildly or moderately depressed, psychological therapies alone may be effective. However, if depression is severe or persists, medication may also be needed.

Antidepressant Medication

There is a great deal of misinformation about antidepressant medication.

Antidepressant medications:

- ARE NOT addictive
- DO NOT change your personality
- DO NOT make people more hostile or aggressive.

Antidepressant medication can play a role when people become severely depressed or when other treatments are ineffective in the treatment of depression. Deciding which antidepressants are best for a person can be complex. There is a range of factors that should be discussed with a doctor before starting antidepressants.

It's important that any current medication or over-the-counter medications including herbal or natural remedies are reviewed by a medical practitioner before a person starts taking antidepressants.

Antidepressant medication can take 14 to 21 days before beginning to work effectively. The prescribing health professional should discuss differences in effects and possible side-effects of medications. Stopping medication should only be done gradually, on a doctor's recommendation and under supervision.

Most people taking medication will also benefit from psychological therapies, which will reduce the likelihood of relapse after the person has stopped taking the medication.

The use of antidepressants in treating young people under the age of 18 should follow the guidelines set out in the National Health and Medical Research Council's *Clinical Practice Guidelines for Depression in Young People* (2011).

Self-help strategies

Any doctor can prescribe antidepressant medication – however, it's important that people try to help themselves to recover and work towards preventing a relapse – with or without medication.

Self-help includes:
- managing thoughts and self-talk
- structured problem-solving
- activity planning and exercise
- reducing alcohol consumption to a moderate level
- managing stress
- restoring a pattern of normal sleep.

The activities in the following pages provide a range of different self-help strategies for managing depression.

What can I do to help someone who is depressed?

People who are depressed are not always easy to help because often, they are disinterested, lack energy and motivation, can be irritable, and may not see the point of doing anything. Some people are not used to talking much – especially about themselves, so even getting a conversation going can be difficult.

Useful tips for helping someone who may be depressed
- Think about the best way to approach the person – given what you know about his/her personality and temperament.
- Discreetly let the person know you have noticed a change in his/her behaviour. Indicate that you are seriously concerned.
- Talk openly about depression and suggest the person visits a doctor, or speaks to a health professional recommended by a doctor.

- If appropriate help the person to make the appointment; perhaps consider going with him/her – and follow up after the appointment.
- If you think the person won't listen to you, consider: Who does this person usually confide in, feel comfortable with, and/or trust? Maybe that person could make the approach and encourage him/her to seek assistance?
- Provide the person with information about depression; give him/her a copy of this book or this section on depression
- Try to find ways of reducing the person's isolation:
  - Make an extra effort to stay in touch, preferably in person.
  - Encourage other close friends and family to do the same.
- Encourage the person to excercise, eat well and become involved in social activities.

It's unhelpful to:
- Pressure people with depression to 'snap out of it', 'get their act together' or 'cheer up'
- Stay away or avoid them
- Tell them they just need to stay busy or get out more
- Pressure them to party more, or to wipe out how they're feeling with drugs or alcohol
- Assume the problem will just go away.
- ➢ Thoughts about self-harm or suicide are serious. Be as determined and resourceful as you can in finding a way to get a person having these thoughts to speak to a doctor or appropriate health professional.

HOW TO TALK TO Someone ABOUT Depression

It's not always easy to know how to help someone who may be experiencing depression. It can be hard to know what to say or do. Here are some tips.

- **Talk to the person** about how he/she is feeling.
- **Listen** to what the person is saying – sometimes, when people want to talk, they're not always seeking advice, but just need to talk about their concerns. Make it clear the person has your full attention and

you are listening properly. You may like to save any suggestions for a later discussion.
- **Maintain eye contact and sit in a relaxed position** – positive body language will help you both feel more comfortable.
- **Use open-ended questions** such as 'So tell me about…?', which require more than a 'yes' or 'no' answer. This is often a good way of starting a conversation.
- **If your conversation becomes difficult** or the person you're talking to gets angry: stay calm; be firm, fair and consistent; admit if you are wrong and don't lose control.
- Often, just **spending time with the person** lets him/her know you care and can help you understand what he/she is going through.
- **Encourage the person to seek professional help** from the family doctor or a mental health worker.
- **Take care of yourself.** Supporting someone with depression can be demanding, so make sure you take some time out to look after yourself.

REMEMBER

➢ Go out of your way and don't give up on them.

➢ Just being with them, being present – even without much talking, can be very supportive and helpful.

MANAGING THOUGHTS AND SELF-TALK

When people become depressed, they often think negatively about **themselves** ("What have I ever achieved?", "I'm no good at anything"), their **circumstances** ("There's no way out of this mess", "It's all pointless…everything I've tried has just made things worse"), and **the future** ("Things will never really change, they'll only get harder").

How we think and what we say to ourselves in our head (self-talk) can have a profound effect on our mood and mental state. It can also cause paralysis in problem-solving and decision-making.

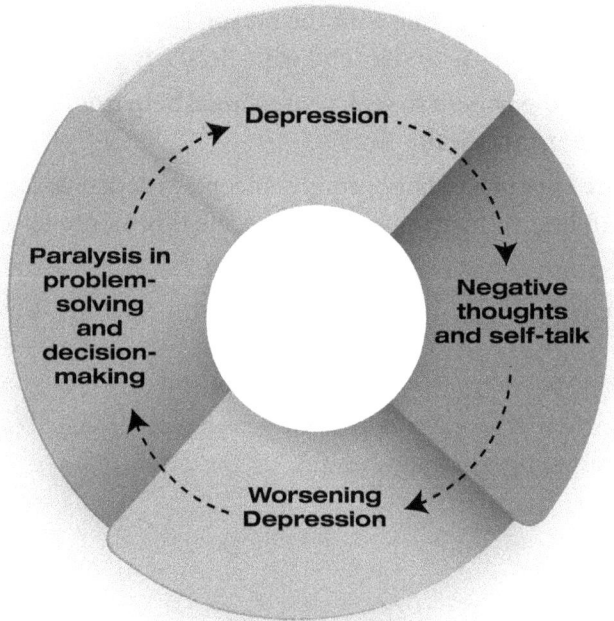

Becoming aware of our thoughts and self-talk, and learning the skill and habit of managing them, is essential to recovery from depression and, later on, preventing relapse.

There are basically two kinds of thought patterns we can use in responding to the things life deals out to us: one that is **Self-Defeating**, because it launches into negative thoughts and self-talk, and one that is **Constructive** and helpful, because it launches into sensible and rational thoughts and self-talk.

Here are some examples:

Self-Defeating Pattern

Situation: Argument with wife

Self-defeating thoughts and self-talk
- *"I can't even get on with my wife anymore"*
- *"Even my marriage is a failure"*
- *"I'm useless at this like everything else"*

Physical Consequences
- Feel 'sick'
- Knot in the stomach
- Feel very tense and shaky

Mental health Consequences
- Worsened depression
- Feel angry and powerless

Behavioural Consequences
- Will give up and withdraw, perhaps even get angry and make things worse

Constructive Pattern

Situation: Argument with wife

Constructive thoughts and self-talk
- *"I don't feel good about this, but we are both tense and on edge"*
- *"Our relationship is OK. We will need to work this through when we are both calm"*

Physical Consequences
- Feel a bit 'wound up' but am becoming calm

Mental health Consequences
- Feel regretful but OK because things are in perspective

Behavioural Consequences
- Will seek to resolve problems in our relationship

Self-defeating interpretations also tend to become more entrenched, and stress or anxiety levels more unhealthy and unhelpful, as a self-reinforcing vicious cycle develops.

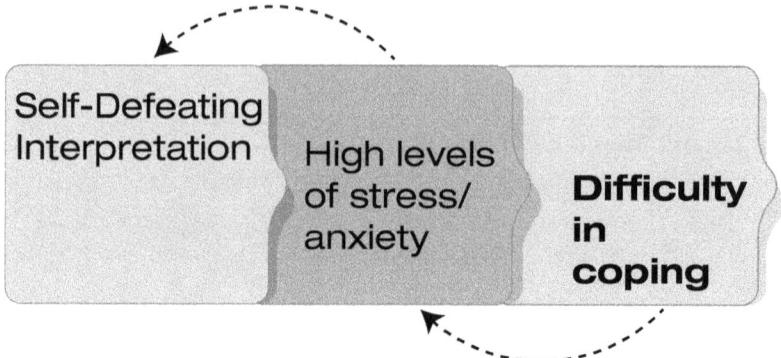

People who tend to use a self-defeating thought pattern in interpreting events also develop (mostly unconsciously) errors in thinking which, like jumping to conclusions, may seem to save time and energy, but can actually have consequences that demand much time and energy.

Adopting a constructive thought pattern in interpreting events is essential for managing stress or anxiety, and for achieving and maintaining good mental health.

How can this be done?

It can be achieved through:

- **becoming aware of how we respond to events** (and what we think and say to ourselves in our heads)
- **censoring and modifying our thoughts** (especially those that are automatic) **and self-talk**
- **challenging and dismantling errors in thinking.**

Becoming aware

We can simply decide to become aware of our thoughts and self-talk. This awareness provides us with the opportunity to change our thoughts and self-talk; it gives us the power of censorship. With practise, it is possible to exert influence over our automatic thoughts (challenging and dismantling errors in thinking will help this too).

To get this awareness underway, it is helpful to do some initial documenting of situations/events to be examined, the feelings experienced, and the thoughts that occur. This is also a good way of identifying errors in thinking.

Situation/event	Feelings experienced	Automatic thoughts (and self-talk)
You discover one of your vehicle tyres is flat, and you were organised to go somewhere.	Immediate 'welling up' of stress and anxiety, then strong feelings of anger.	"Everything just has to go wrong, like everything else around this place. I just don't need this."
Situation/event	Feelings experienced	Automatic thoughts (and self-talk)

Practising taking 'snapshots' of situations, and writing things down like this, is a useful tool for establishing awareness. After a while, this can be expanded into the skill of *censoring and modifying* thoughts and self-talk.

Censoring and modifying

The key to censoring and modifying (or managing) thoughts and self-talk is the speed with which we intervene and ask ourselves: Is this thought/idea (or what I've begun saying to myself) self-defeating or constructive? If it is self-defeating, how can I modify it immediately or replace it, so that I am using a constructive mental pattern?

This is a skill to be practised and a new habit to be formed. As with becoming *aware*, it can be really helpful (at least initially), to write things down; when we can 'see' our thoughts and what we are saying to ourselves, we have more power to change them.

LEARNING TO MANAGE THOUGHTS

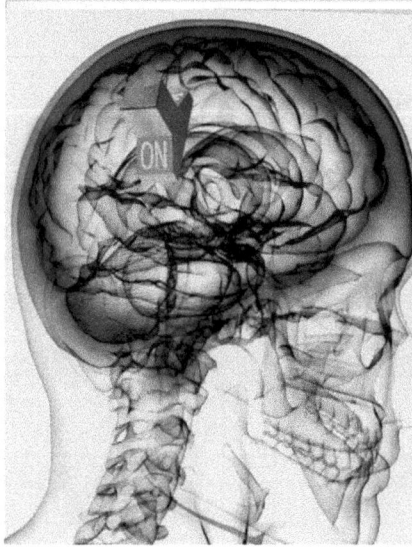

- ✓ Thinking rationally about challenges and problems
- ✓ Using structured problem solving
- ✓ Avoiding catastrophising
- ✓ 'Nipping in the bud' negative thinking
- ✓ Finding distractions when negative thinking occurs

Situation/event	My thoughts and self-talk	Are these self-defeating or constructive?	If self-defeating, what would be constructive?
A friend, who you had arranged to come over and help you with something important, has left a message to cancel.	"Why is it me that gets let down? This is typical of the way things go for me. One of these days something might just go right."	Self-defeating, because I have reacted negatively and feel more flat and depressed than before.	Considering: How do I know why he had to cancel? It could have been an emergency. I've cancelled things too. There are other things I can do; this can be put on hold. Everyone feels let down sometimes — that's life.
Situation/event	My thoughts and self-talk	Are these self-defeating or constructive?	If self-defeating, what would be constructive?
Situation/event	My thoughts and self-talk	Are these self-defeating or constructive?	If self-defeating, what would be constructive?

Challenging and dismantling errors in thinking

Errors in thinking consist of certain assumptions and ways of thinking that keep recurring, are habitual, and allow us to save time by not thinking *constructively* about events. They provide an easy response, but one that is neither time-saving nor helpful. Errors in thinking 'save a penny and spend a pound,' because their consequences heavily tax our energy reserves, and generate high and unhealthy levels of stress or anxiety.

Errors in thinking need to be challenged and revised if we are to establish a constructive and healthy mental thought pattern.

EXAMPLES OF COMMON ERRORS IN THINKING

Assumptions	Challenge
All things are equally important and urgent.	Many things are not crucial or urgent. But they generate anxiety because I interpret them that way. Some things are crucial and/or urgent and cannot be left. Many things are not, and they can be postponed.
Getting uptight about unforeseen or unwanted events is inevitable.	If I'm stressed or anxious, what does a thing matter, unless it is truly crucial or urgent? Getting up tight is not inevitable or necessary, it is a habit. Lots of other people take these things pretty much in their stride. No, getting uptight often is mostly because I often interpret events in a self-defeating way.

Assumptions	Challenge
Everything has to go wrong. Life is against me succeeding.	Based on what evidence? What about people who, against all apparent odds, still succeed?
	Do I need to examine how I go about things – how I make decisions, and for what reasons?
	If I expect things to go wrong, isn't it highly likely I will contribute to that happening? Has 'life' really singled me out to be a victim?
People always let me down.	What real evidence supports this assumption?
	Are other people let down also? How does my experience compare with theirs?
	Have I on occasions let others down?
	Do I know anyone who always experiences other people as completely reliable?
	Do I automatically believe the best or the worst when people appear to let me down? Are my expectations reasonable?

Assumptions	Challenge
If I could go back in time: If I had... If only I did...	The benefit of hindsight is a fine thing. Of course I could be more knowledgeable, skilled and wise if I could have been then who I am now, or if I could go back as who I am now. How is this kind of thinking helpful? I was who I was. I made decisions and did things as the person I was, and was capable of being **then**. No amount of lamenting will change that. The only valid questions are perhaps: What can I learn from the past? What can I do differently now and in the future?
Everything has to be done perfectly or properly	No one could live up to that, without lying about the many occasions when they, quite rightly, didn't bother to do some things either perfectly or properly. Taking pride in doing important things well is admirable. But trying to do everything perfectly or properly is not necessary, important, reasonable, or admirable. It is plain unhealthy! Perhaps what is more needful is to be able to prioritise?

Other thinking habits:

Mind-reading:	"She thinks I'm a failure;" "They think I'm not as good as…"
Catastrophising:	"Everything always turns out bad for me;" "Things are always against me;" "Now I will never be able to…;" "No matter how hard I try everything always goes wrong."
Labelling:	"I'm an idiot;" "I'm a failure;" "I'm a lousy…" (Instead of "I did… poorly;" or "I did not achieve…;" or "I needed to…")
Over-generalising:	Saying, "Always," "Never," "No-one," or "Everyone."
Fortune-telling:	"Everyone is sure to…;" "I'm sure to mess it up;" "It's going to be a disaster;" "I'm sure to feel dreadful when I…"
Rule-saying:	"Should," "Must," or "Have to" (setting sometimes unrealistic expectations).
Black and white thinking:	"Everything she does she gets right;" "I've completely ruined everything;" "He succeeds in everything… I never get it right!"

Examples you can think of:

....

....

....

....

STRUCTURED PROBLEM-SOLVING

It's common for people who are depressed to feel stressed and overwhelmed by problems. Adopting a new way of tackling problems can be very helpful.

Structured problem-solving is a method designed to help you feel in control of your problems, and to enable you to deal more effectively with future problems.

The **key elements** of this method include:

- Identifying and 'pinning down' the problems that have contributed to you feeling overwhelmed
- Thinking clearly and constructively about problems
- 'Taking stock' of how you've coped in the past: your personal strengths, and the support and resources available to you
- Providing a sound basis for important decision-making.

With this method, you can work on a single problem or follow the process to tackle a number of problems.

Usually though, it's best to deal with one problem that is specific and potentially solvable – especially to begin with.

STRUCTURED PROBLEM – SOLVING INVOLVES 6 STEPS

STEP 1 Write down the problem causing you worry or distress:

STEP 2 Think about your options for dealing with this problem (try to think broadly – including good and not so good options); write them down:

1.	
2.	
3.	
4.	
5.	

STEP 3 Write down the advantages and disadvantages of each option:

STEP 4 Identify the best option(s) to deal with the problem:

1.	
2.	
3.	
4.	
5.	

STEP 5

List the steps needed to carry out each option (bear in mind the resources needed and pitfalls to overcome):

1. a.
b.
c.
2. a.
b.
c.
3. a.
b.
c.
4. a.
b.
c.
5. a.
b.
c.

STEP 6

Review your progress in carrying out your option(s):

What have I achieved? ....

....

What still needs to be done? ....

....

ACTIVITY PLANNING

Many people who have depression experience a loss of energy, motivation, interest and pleasure in things previously meaningful or enjoyed.

As a result, they become less physically, mentally, and socially active – which tends to worsen depression. Becoming active again is an important step in breaking the cycle of depression.

Activity planning aims to break the cycle of depression by methodically and gradually restoring important daily activities.

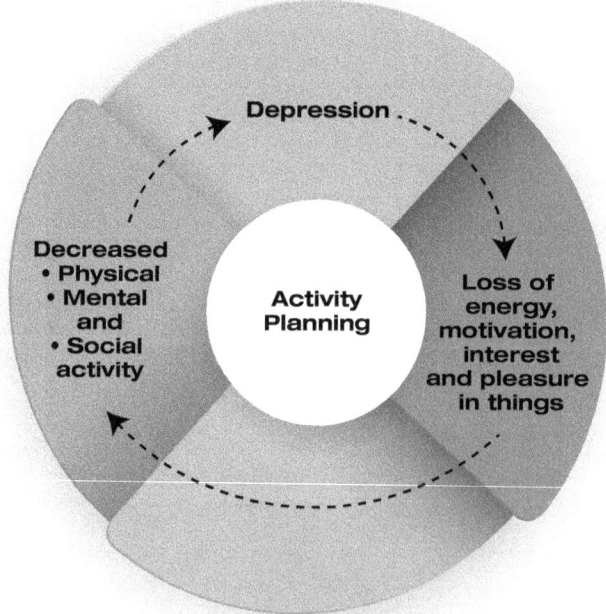

ACHIEVEMENT ACTIVITIES

Daily achievements, even if only small, can help restore the lost experience of meaning and satisfaction; they can also reverse the sense of paralysis that is so common with depression.

List the activities that previously gave you a sense of achievement:

Number in order of importance

- .... ☐
- .... ☐
- .... ☐
- .... ☐
- .... ☐

List work tasks that need to be done, which will give you a sense of achievement or relief to complete:

Number in order of importance

- .... ☐
- .... ☐
- .... ☐
- .... ☐
- .... ☐

SOCIAL ACTIVITIES

People who are depressed commonly withdraw from family, friends, and important social activities. Social isolation, which can quickly set in, only serves to worsen depression and make recovery more difficult.

Doing things with other people, even if it doesn't feel comfortable at first (and even if you have to drive a long distance), can help motivate you, lift your mood, and improve your general state of mind. It is important to decide to accept social invitations and to pursue opportunities for social contact and activities.

List the social contact and activities that used to be important to you:

Number in order of importance

- .... ☐
- .... ☐
- .... ☐
- .... ☐

List the family and friends you need to reconnect with or spend more time with:

Number in order of importance

- .... ☐
- .... ☐
- .... ☐
- .... ☐

Pleasant Activities

People who are depressed often lose interest and pleasure in things they once liked doing.

It is vital to recovery from depression, to plan activities that can again be a source of enjoyment, pleasure and satisfaction.

List activities that you would normally find enjoyable, interesting relaxing or satisfying:

Number in order of importance

- .... ☐
- .... ☐
- .... ☐
- .... ☐

Physical Activities

Regular daily exercise can be a powerful antidote for depression. Ideally this should be done early in the day and in the sunlight. Certainly, manual work provides exercise; but the best kind of physical activity for depression is separate from work, and purely dedicated to improving physical and mental health. Walking, cycling, using weights or an exercise machine, for example, even if only for 15 minutes a day, can be quite beneficial.

Bearing in mind any medical condition or physical limitations you might have, list physical/exercise activities you have done in the past:

Select one of these to recommence

- .... ☐
- .... ☐
- .... ☐
- .... ☐

Now that you have listed and prioritised all the activities that are important for your recovery from depression: **Achievement, Social, Pleasant,** and **Physical Activities,** put your number one selections into your diary (or Daily Activities Diary provided).

Tips for Successful Activities Planning

- Whenever possible put one of each of these activities into your diary each day.
- 'Don't bite off more than you can chew;' better to achieve small goals than to feel a failure because of attempting too much.
- If you start an activity or task and 'run out of steam,' or for some other reason can't commence it or complete it, that's fine. Simply reschedule it for the next day or another suitable time.
- Try to be sure you have the day's activity plan completed the evening before, or in advance, so that you have a plan of action to follow immediately when you get up.

DAILY ACTIVITIES DIARY

Time	SUNDAY	MONDAY	TUESDAY	WEDNESDAY
8.00am				
9.00am				
10.00am				
11.00am				
12.00noon				
1.00pm				
2.00pm				
3.00pm				
4.00pm				
5.00pm				
6.00pm				
7.00pm				
8.00pm				
9.00pm				
10.00pm				

DAILY ACTIVITIES DIARY Continued

Time	THURSDAY	FRIDAY	SATURDAY
8.00am			
9.00am			
10.00am			
11.00am			
12.00noon			
1.00pm			
2.00pm			
3.00pm			
4.00pm			
5.00pm			
6.00pm			
7.00pm			
8.00pm			
9.00pm			
10.00pm			

REDUCING ALCOHOL CONSUMPTION TO A MODERATE LEVEL

Many people 'drown their sorrows' and try to escape problems and feelings of depression through the use of alcohol.

The problem is that any relief alcohol does provide is short-lived. Alcohol is actually a depressant drug – it spoils the quality of sleep and interferes with the effects of antidepressant medication.

Strategies for moderating drinking

- Try to avoid drinking at home alone – especially when you are feeling down or anxious.
- Try limiting your drinking to the evening meal time.
- Drink low-alcohol beers and mixes.
- Drink slowly (limit yourself to 2 standard drinks each day).
- Think ahead (and creatively) about how to avoid drinking excessively in situations (like the pub or social gatherings) where there is pressure to do so.
- Use your Daily Activity Diary to plan two alcohol-free days each week. Try to choose days when it is easiest to do so; like when an activity is planned for the evening that can be a useful distraction.
- Decide beforehand how much alcohol you will permit yourself to drink; measure it out, and only allow yourself that amount.
- Always try to stay within the **Australian Alcohol Guidelines.**

For Men and Women

Over a lifetime: If you drink no more than 2 standard drinks a day, you reduce the lifetime risk of harming yourself from alcohol-related disease or injury.

On a single occasion: Having no more than 4 standard drinks on a single occasion reduces the risk of alcohol-related injury arising from that occasion.

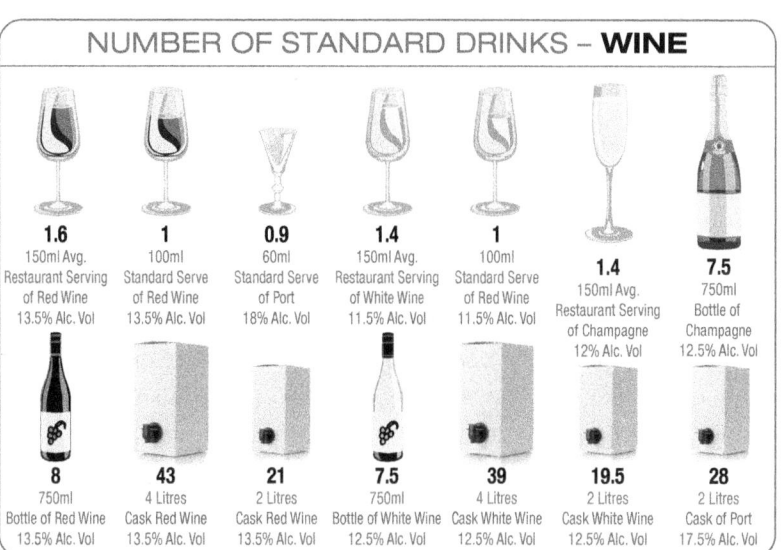

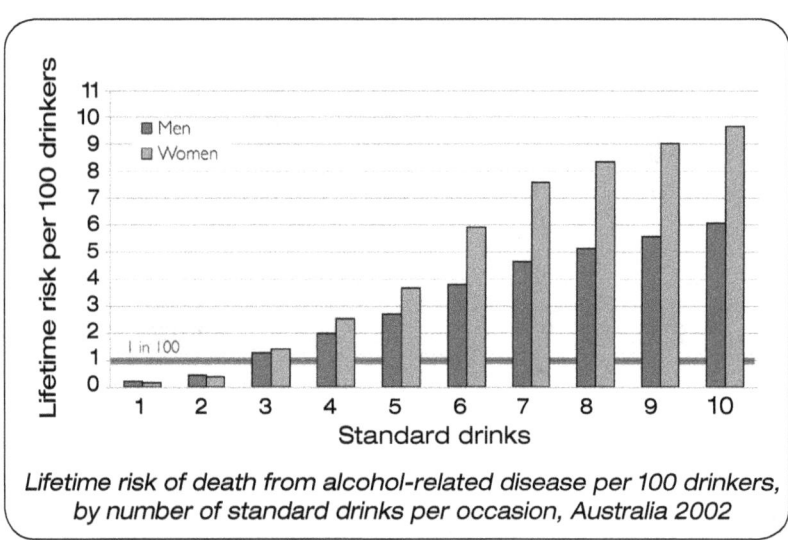

Lifetime risk of death from alcohol-related disease per 100 drinkers, by number of standard drinks per occasion, Australia 2002

For people who regularly drink 2 standard drinks per day, the lifetime risk of death from an alcohol-related disease is about 0.4 in 100 people with that drinking pattern. Above that level, the risk increases with the number of drinks per day, and is above 1 in 100 at 3 drinks per day. The risk increases more sharply for women than for men.

Source: National Health and Medical Research Council Australian Guidelines to Reduce Health Risks from Drinking Alcohol, Canberra: Commonwealth of Australia, 2009.

MANAGING STRESS

Emotional stress and acute distress have been identified as significant contributing factors to depression. However, trying to create a stress-free life would be both unrealistic and undesirable, since stress is associated with work, family and personal relationships – in fact with nearly all the changes and challenges that enable us to develop, adapt, and make our way successfully through life.

The problem arises when we experience too much stress – particularly at one time. For people who are depressed, too many sources of stress (or *stressors*) can worsen and prolong their depression. Consequently, finding ways of reducing and managing stress may be very important.

Ways of reducing stress

- **Postponing major life changes**

  Some major life changes may be unavoidable. But it is best to postpone changes that are likely to generate stress and upheaval, if possible.

- **Learning to relax**

  Think of the things that help you relax, and set aside time in the day to do more of them. Also, be sure to get enough rest and sleep each day.

- **Regular daily exercise**

  Find a form of gentle exercise (apart from work) that you enjoy and can keep doing on a regular basis.

- **Learn to say no and set priorities**

  You may need to say "no" more often to new commitments, and instead concentrate on your activities plan.

- **Work on your relationship**

  One of the most common contributors to long-term depression is tension and conflict in personal relationships. You may need to devote more time to 'greasing the gears' and resolving issues in your relationships. If you have access to a skilled counsellor, that could help a lot. If not, there are useful self-help books available in book stores and libraries, and information on the internet.

- **Use Financial Advisory Services or Rural Counselling**

  Financial difficulties can be hugely stressful and are one of the leading causes of relationship breakdown. Using the expertise and more objective view of a financial advisor or rural counsellor can make a very real difference to how people view and tackle financial hardship or pressure. Even when there appear to be no easy solutions, getting things into perspective, being clear about options, and getting a chance (perhaps for the first time) to speak about how difficult things are, can significantly reduce feelings of powerlessness and stress.

  Rural Financial Counsellor Coordinators:
  Central NSW - 0407 282 843
  Northern NSW - 02 6662 5055
  Southern NSW - 02 6452 3766
  Northern QLD - 07 4652 5666
  Southern QLD - 07 4622 5500
  Eastern VIC - 03 5662 2566
  North Eastern VIC - 1300 834 775
  North Western VIC - 1300 769 489
  Western VIC - 1300 735 578
  SA - NT - 1800 836 211
  TAS - 1300 88 3276
  WA - 1800 612 004

  Financial Counselling Australia:
  www.financialcounsellingaustralia.org.au
  to find a service in your area

RESTORING A NORMAL PATTERN OF SLEEP

Sleep disturbance is common with depression, and frequently takes the form of early-morning wakening (usually around 3am) with difficulty returning to sleep. To restore a normal pattern of sleep, it's important to practise sleep-promoting behaviour during the day, in the evening, at bedtime, and during the night.

Better Sleep Guidelines
During the Day
- Organise your day. Regular times for eating meals, taking medicines, performing chores and other activities, help keep our inner clocks running smoothly.
- Regular exercise during the day (or early evening) can improve sleeping patterns.
- Set aside time for problem-solving and decision-making during the day, to avoid worry or anxiety at night.
- Avoid napping during the day, go to bed and get up at regular times.

During the Evening
- Put the day to rest. If you still have things on your mind, write them down or put them in your Daily Activities Diary, to be dealt with tomorrow.
- Light exercise early in the evening may help sleep. Avoid exercise late in the evening, as this may make getting to sleep more difficult.
- Get into a routine of 'winding down' during the course of the evening, allowing at least half an hour of quiet activity, such as reading or listening to music, prior to bedtime.
- Avoid drinking caffeinated drinks after about 4pm, and don't drink more than 2 cups of caffeinated drinks each day (especially coffee, tea, cocoa, and cola).
- Avoid smoking for at least an hour (preferably an hour and a half) before going to bed.
- Don't use alcohol to make you sleep, and keep your intake moderate (limit yourself to 2 standard drinks each day). Have 1 or 2 alcohol-free days each week.

- Make sure your bed and bedroom are comfortable – not too cold or too warm.
- Ensure that your bedroom is dark and that the morning light does not filter in. However, if you have a tendency to oversleep, it may be helpful to let the morning light into the room.
- Avoid a heavy meal close to bedtime. If you are hungry, a light snack may help you get to sleep.

At Bedtime

- Try to do the same things before you go to bed each night.

  Develop a calming bedtime routine, such as having a warm bath or shower, listening to relaxation music, or using a relaxation technique. This way your body will learn to know that (with these activities) you are getting ready to go to sleep.
- Go to bed when you feel 'sleepy tired' and not before.
- Don't watch TV or have conversations or arguments in bed. Keep your bed and bedroom only for sleep (and sexual activity).
- Turn the light off when you get into bed.
- Relax and tell yourself that sleep will come when it is ready.

  Enjoy relaxing your mind and body, even if you don't fall asleep at first.

During the Night

- If you wake up too early in the night, don't lie awake for more than 30 minutes. Instead of just being awake or worrying, get out of bed and do something that is distracting yet relaxing. Return to bed only when you feel sleepy again.
- Get up at the same time each morning. Don't sleep late in the morning trying to make up for 'lost sleep.'
- If you live in a place or area where there are sounds or noises that might wake you from sleep, use earplugs to block out the noise.
- Avoid sleeping pills - they do not provide a long-term solution to sleep problems.

WARNING SIGNS OF ANXIETY

Tick ☑ the signs that are familiar:

- ❑ Feeling 'on edge' or 'wound up' much of the time
- ❑ Constantly worried about a lot of things
- ❑ Feeling irritable frequently
- ❑ Tense or nervous much of the time
- ❑ Avoiding people and social situations
- ❑ Trembling, tingling, light-headedness, dizzy spells, sweating, urinary frequency, diarrhoea
- ❑ Feeling panicky in some situations
- ❑ Sleeping poorly/having difficulty falling asleep
- ❑ Having difficulty relaxing
- ❑ Fear of making a fool of yourself socially, or of other people watching you or drawing attention to you
- ❑ Using alcohol or sedatives to calm down or to get to sleep
- ❑ Fear of having a serious illness that the doctor can't detect
- ❑ Fear of experiencing again the feelings of a past traumatic event
- ❑ Worrying a lot about your health
- ❑ Fear of dying, going mad, or having something bad happen
- ❑ Having thoughts that are hard to control
- ❑ Fear of being in a place that you can't get out of, or that you can't get out of without embarrassment
- ❑ Fear of germs or infection
- ❑ Compulsively checking, counting or cleaning things
- ❑ Headaches, neck aches, chest pain, joint pain, or nausea
- ❑ Tiredness or fatigue

If you have some of these symptoms and
they are affecting your life –

TAKE ACTION
Arrange to speak to a doctor

ABOUT ANXIETY

The 'Fight or Flight' response

Most people experiencing problems with anxiety visit their doctor because of worrying physical symptoms. It is important to understand that the symptoms of anxiety, rather than suggesting evidence of an underlying physical problem, are actually the result of what has been termed the 'fight or flight' response.

When we are threatened by something or are in danger, our bodies respond with a series of biochemical changes aimed at preparing us to fight or escape. This harks back to our more primitive past, when people frequently needed quick bursts of energy, as their bodies prepared to fight off or flee from ferocious predators or enemies. This remains an important response when we are faced with a real threat or danger. The problem is, our brain (in activating the 'fight or flight' response) does not distinguish between what is real or what is imagined.

Many novice public speakers would confess that giving a speech – even to a sympathetic audience – can generate as much terror and anxiety as any real physical danger or threat. What we imagine or perceive as threatening, and the way we anticipate problems or challenges in the future, whether real or not, may be 'real' enough for our brain to activate a response.

Mild to moderate levels of anxiety – of 'fight or flight' arousal – are normal, and can energise us, improve our thinking, reactions, and general performance. Too much anxiety, especially if it is prolonged, has the opposite and negative effect of diminishing our ability to cope and interfering with our lives.

Changes that occur due to the 'Fight or Flight' response

- The mind becomes alert.
- Blood clotting ability increases, preparing for possible injury.
- Heart rate speeds up and blood pressure rises.
- Sweating increases to help cool the body.
- Blood is diverted to the muscles which tense ready for action.
- Digestion slows down.
- Saliva production decreases causing a dry mouth.
- Breathing rate speeds up – nostrils and air passages in lungs open wider to get in air more quickly.
- Liver releases sugar to provide quick energy.
- Sphincter muscles contract to close the openings of the bowel and bladder.
- Immune responses decrease (which is useful in the short-term to allow massive response to immediate threat, but can become harmful over a long period).
- Trembling or shaking
- Restlessness
- Cold and clammy hands
- Hot flushes or chills
- Feeling sick or nauseous
- Butterflies in the stomach

Excerpt from: **Management of Mental Disorders** Third edition (Australia, World Health Organization Collaborating Centre For Mental Health And Substance Abuse, 2000) Volumes 1 & 2.

Brain activates fight or flight response

Situation or event that is perceived as dangerous or threatening

ANXIETY

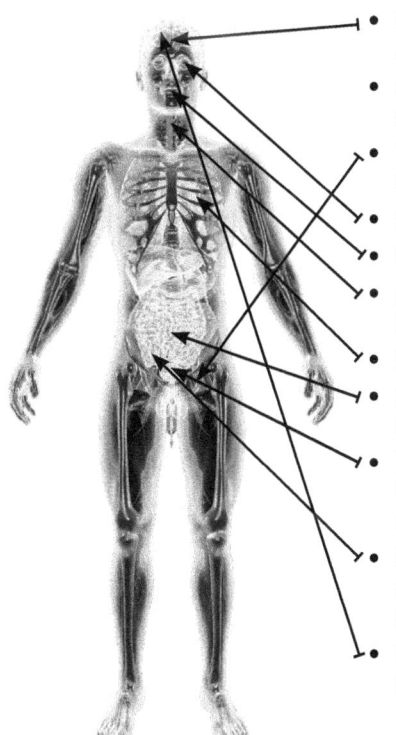

- Perceiving a threat, our primitive Amygdala sounds a general alarm.
- Our entire body is put in a state of high alert ready for fight or flight.
- The Adrenal system floods the body with adrenaline and stress hormones.
- Pupils dilate to better signal danger.
- Salivation is inhibited.
- Airways are relaxed – taking in more oxygen.
- Blood pressure and heart rate spike.
- Stomach and gastrointestinal tract constrict to divert blood to muscles.
- Bladder and colon prepare to void their contents in preparation for violent action and possible injury.
- Spleen contracts, pumping out white blood cells and platelets in preparation for potential physical injury.
- Hippocampus cements the response to the threat into long-term memory.

ANXIETY CONDITIONS

Anxiety of a kind that is seriously disruptive to people's lives can take a number of different forms, each with a range of symptoms. Common anxiety conditions include:

Generalised Anxiety

People who have GA feel anxious on most days for at least six months. Generally, they worry about real issues such as finances, illness or family problems – to the point where it interferes with functioning from day to day.

Phobia

When a person has a phobia, he/she feels very fearful about particular objects or situations. Common examples include fear of social situations such as parties and meetings (social phobia) or fear of open spaces such as parks and big shopping centres (agoraphobia).

Obsessive Compulsive Anxiety

Obsessive Compulsive Anxiety gets its name because people who experience it have ongoing unwanted/intrusive thoughts and fears that cause anxiety called *obsessions*. These obsessions make people feel they need to carry out certain rituals in order to feel less anxious and these rituals are known as *compulsions*. Common obsessions may include fear of forgetting to do things, fear of germs/contamination, whereas compulsions may include constant checking behaviour and constant washing of hands.

Panic Attacks/Episodes

A panic attack is an intense feeling of anxiety that is overwhelming and difficult to manage. Panic attacks have been likened to the experience of having a heart attack and may include shortness of breath, feeling lightheaded and/or nauseous or having chest pains.

Acute Stress and Post-Traumatic Stress

AS and PTS are a set of reactions that can develop in people who have experienced or witnessed a traumatic event. Traumatic events involve life-threatening situations or serious injury that lead to feelings of intense fear, helplessness or horror, e.g. assault, war, serious accident, natural disaster.

Anxiety can be very disabling

In a recent Australian Bureau of Statistics survey, around 1 in 7 people indicated that they were experiencing symptoms consistent with an anxiety difficulty. People with anxiety difficulties reported being unable to carry out their usual roles and tasks.

People with anxiety difficulties are also at increased risk of developing depression (2-4 times higher than people without a history of anxiety). Anxiety difficulties pre-date depression in most cases and more often than not, anxiety and depression are found together when depression is diagnosed.

What if anxiety is left untreated?

Left untreated, a problem of anxiety is likely to continue and worsen with significant life-diminishing consequences. As already mentioned, people with moderate to severe anxiety problems are at increased risk of developing depression.

The outlook for people with anxiety who do receive treatment is generally very good. But, just as with depression, people with anxiety will need to be actively involved in their treatment, mastering new skills and adopting changes in lifestyle.

WHAT ARE THE TREATMENTS FOR ANXIETY?

For mild to severe anxiety health difficulties, psychological therapy is the basis of treatment. Medication may sometimes be useful, especially for severe anxiety, or when there are repeated episodes of panic or obsessional thinking.

Medication

One of the most common medications used to treat anxiety is also used to treat depression. Its technical name is Selective Serotonin Reuptake Inhibitor (SSRI). SSRIs are also frequently used when anxiety and depression appear together.

Psychological Therapy

Even when drugs are prescribed, psychological therapy is an indispensable part of treatment. The therapies and strategies widely used and found to be most helpful for treating anxiety difficulties include:

- **controlled breathing**
- **relaxation**
- **adopting constructive thought patterns**
- **structured problem-solving**
- **restoring a pattern of normal sleep**
- **graded exposure**
- **reducing alcohol and caffeine consumption.**

If a suitable health professional is unavailable in your area, you may access therapy online.

Your doctor may recommend the use of medication and the self-help version of these therapies (along with other strategies) mentioned in this resource book.

Though these self-help 'therapies' do reflect (and are a simplified form of) the therapies used by trained psychotherapists, they are not intended as a substitute for seeing a doctor, or for psychological therapy when that is what the doctor strongly recommends. In the case of a severe anxiety difficulty (especially if it has particularly difficult features), it may be recommended and necessary to travel to where psychological therapy is available.

Controlled Breathing

The 'fight or flight' response associated with anxiety creates an increase in the rate of breathing. This increase may constitute over-breathing (called hyperventilation) which may give rise to a whole range of symptoms:

> **Some of the symptoms of over-breathing**
> - Light-headedness
> - Blurred vision
> - Feeling strange
> - Increased heartbeat
> - Stiffness, twitching, or cramps in muscles
> - Breathlessness
> - Confusion
> - Irregular heartbeat
> - Cold, clammy hands
> - Numbness and tingling in hands or feet
>
> Because over-breathing is hard physical work, a person may feel:
> - Hot, flushed and sweaty
> - Tired and exhausted
>
> Over-breathing may over-use chest muscles resulting in:
> - Chest tightness
> - Severe chest pain

Over-breathing is not always obvious to the observer or even to anxious people themselves. It can be very subtle – especially if the individual has been slightly over-breathing for a long period of time. Mild over-breathing can cause a person to be in a constant state of fearfulness and anxiety.

Over-breathing is especially associated with the experience of panic and may act as the initial prompt causing an individual to panic.

One proven way of managing and reducing the symptoms of over-breathing is by using a controlled or slow breathing technique.

> **Controlled Breathing Technique**
> 1. Breathe in (without taking a deep breath) and hold your breath for a count of 4.
> 2. When you get to 4, gently breathe out saying to yourself "relax" or "calm".
> 3. Then just breathe in and out slowly, through your nose, counting 3 with each breath in, and 3 with each breath out.
> 4. Breathe this way for about 10 breaths, and then start the cycle again by holding your breath and counting to 4 (step 1).
> 5. Continue this controlled breathing cycle until all the symptoms of over-breathing have gone.

Tips on the use of the Controlled Breathing Technique

- Use the technique immediately the first signs of over-breathing, panic, or growing anxiety occur.
- Practise the technique at least 4 times each day.
- 'Over-learn' the technique (practise it until it becomes an automatic response), so that it can be used quickly to prevent anxiety escalating.
- Spend enough time practising the technique for it to feel comfortable.

Relaxation

The same mechanism that turns on the anxiety response can also switch it off again. When we decide to let go of physical and mental tension (and take steps to do so), the nerves in our muscles change the type of signals they transmit to the brain. The brain then stops sending panic messages to our nervous system, and a general feeling of calmness, both physical and mental, begins to prevail. The *relaxation response* can help switch off the fight or flight anxiety response.

For people who are often anxious, there is little opportunity for high levels of muscle tension to diminish. The consequence of living with a high level of tension is that a *state of tension* becomes 'normal' and is taken for granted – so that being tense isn't noticed.

Becoming aware of tension in our body, and taking steps to release it through effective relaxation, is a vital strategy in the management of anxiety.

Recognising Tension

Ask yourself these questions:
- Where do I feel tension?
  - In which parts of my body?
  - In which muscles?
- What does the tension feel like?
  - Is there hardness?
  - Is there fatigue?
  - Is there an ache or pain?
- What is it that has led to this tension?
- Is this tension helpful or unhelpful?
- Do I need to make time to relax?

Progressive Muscle Relaxation

A method of relaxation with proven effectiveness which relieves muscle tension, and can help switch off the 'fight or flight' anxiety response, is progressive muscle relaxation. This involves tensing and then relaxing muscles in a step-by-step sequence. The two main principles of this technique include:

1. Tensing muscle groups (one at a time) to become aware of the feeling of tension.
2. Relaxing the muscles and feeling the tension in them subside – as if flowing out of the body.

Progressive Muscle Relaxation

- You will need about 15 minutes for this relaxation exercise.
- Find a quiet place where you won't be interrupted.
- Sit in a comfortable straight-backed chair, with your feet flat on the floor.
- Close your eyes and use the controlled breathing technique for about 5 minutes.
- Tense each of the following muscle groups for 5 seconds, then relax them completely for 15-20 seconds (pay particular attention to the different sensations of tension and relaxation):

    1. Curl both your fists and tighten your biceps and forearms (as if lifting weights). Relax.
    2. Wrinkle up your forehead; tighten the muscles in your face causing your face to wrinkle; purse your lips and press your tongue against the roof of your mouth; hunch your shoulders. Relax.
    3. Arch your back as you take a deep breath into your chest. Relax.
    4. Taking a deep breath, gently push out your stomach. Relax.
    5. Pull your feet and toes backwards tightening your shins. Relax.
    6. Curl your toes at the same time as tightening your calves, thighs and buttocks. Relax.

- Close your eyes and use the controlled breathing technique for about 5 minutes.
- Now resume normal activities in a calm and peaceful manner.

Tips and cautions on the use of progressive muscle relaxation

- Be patient with yourself and this technique. You may only experience partial success at first. In time, it should be possible for you to relax your whole body quickly and successfully. Practise is the key.
- Be careful when you are tensing your neck and back. Don't tighten your muscles beyond what feels comfortable for you.
- To achieve the best results with this technique it's important to let go of the tension in a group of muscles you have tensed instantly. Releasing tension slowly may seem to relax muscles, when in fact it may just sustain tension. When you release muscle tension, do it instantly and let the muscles suddenly become limp.

Other relaxation techniques

There are many relaxation techniques that people find helpful, such as meditation, yoga, self-hypnosis and relaxation music combined with guided imagery or visualisation.

ADOPTING A CONSTRUCTIVE THOUGHT PATTERN

What we perceive as dangerous or threatening activates the 'fight or flight' response. When this perception changes – either because the danger or threat ceases, or because we alter the way we think about or interpret it ("this is not a threat or danger to me"), the 'fight or flight' response is deactivated or turned off.

How we interpret life events (the things that happen to us, challenge us, make demands of us, or that we perceive may have consequences for us), has a huge bearing on how much stress or anxiety we experience.

Part of this interpreting is what we think, how we think and what we say to ourselves in our head (our self-talk).

The kind of thought pattern or way of interpreting events that we use is generally either **self-defeating** or, alternatively, **constructive**.

Self-defeating interpretations (thoughts and self-talk) can generate high and unhealthy levels of stress or anxiety – as well as causing paralysis in attempts at problem-solving and decision-making.

Constructive interpretations (thoughts and self-talk) help to maintain healthy and useful levels of stress or anxiety, which permit and promote coping.

Self-defeating interpretations also tend to become more entrenched, and stress or anxiety levels more unhealthy and unhelpful, as a self-reinforcing vicious cycle develops.

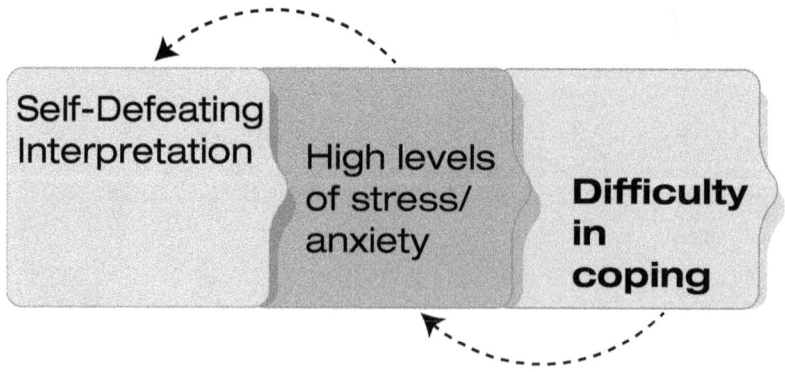

Self-Defeating Interpretation

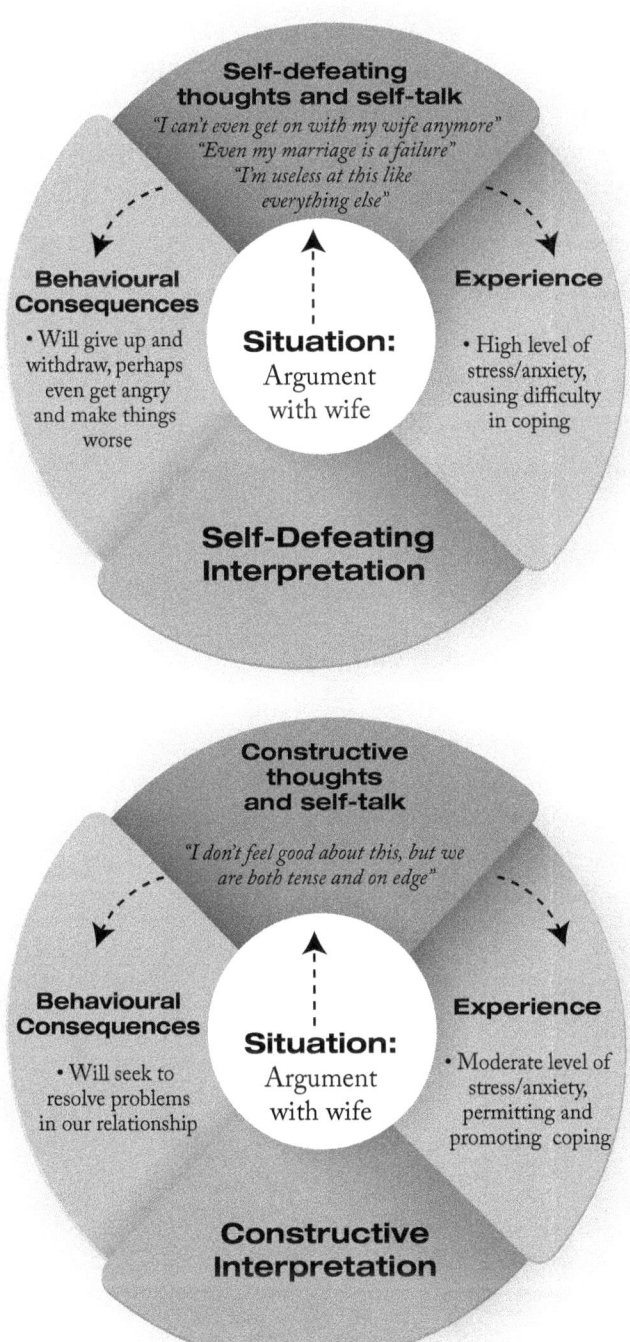

People who tend to use a self-defeating thought pattern in interpreting events also develop (mostly unconsciously) *errors* in thinking which, like 'jumping to conclusions,' may seem to save time and energy, but can actually have consequences that demand much time and energy.

Adopting a constructive thought pattern in interpreting events is essential for managing stress or anxiety, and for achieving and maintaining good mental health.

How can this be done? It can be achieved through:
- **becoming aware of how we respond to events**
  (and what we think and say to ourselves in our heads)
- **censoring and modifying our thoughts**
  (especially those that are automatic) and self-talk
- **challenging and dismantling errors in thinking.**

Becoming aware

We can simply decide to become aware of our thoughts and self-talk. This awareness provides us with the opportunity to change them; it gives us the power of censorship. With practise, it's possible to even exert influence over our automatic thoughts (challenging and dismantling errors in thinking will help this too).

To get this awareness underway, it's helpful to do some initial documenting of situations/events to be examined, the feelings experienced and the thoughts that occur. This is also a good way of identifying errors in thinking.

Situation/event	Feelings experienced	Automatic thoughts (and self-talk)
You discover one of your vehicle tyres is flat, and you were organised to go somewhere.	Immediate 'welling up' of stress and anxiety, then strong feelings of anger.	"Everything just has to go wrong, like everything else around this place. I just don't need this."
Situation/event	Feelings experienced	Automatic thoughts (and self-talk)

Practising taking 'snapshots' of situations and writing things down like this, is a useful tool for establishing awareness. After a while this can be expanded into the skill of *censoring and modifying* thoughts and self-talk.

Censoring and modifying

The key to censoring and modifying (or managing) thoughts and self-talk is the speed with which we intervene and ask ourselves: Is this thought/idea (or what I've begun saying to myself) self-defeating or constructive? If it is self-defeating, how can I immediately modify it or replace it so that I am using a constructive thought pattern?

This is a skill to be practised and a new habit to be formed. As with *becoming aware*, it can be really helpful (at least initially), to write things down; when we can 'see' our thoughts and what we are saying to ourselves, we have more power to change them.

ANXIETY

Situation/event	My thoughts and self-talk	Are these self-defeating or constructive?	If self-defeating, what would be constructive?
A friend, who you had arranged to come over and help you with something important, has left a message to cancel.	Great! Thanks a lot! Why is it I always get let down?	Self-defeating, because I can feel stress and anger building up.	How do I know why he cancelled…it could have been an emergency? Everyone feels let down sometimes, that's life. I've cancelled things too. There are other things I can do; this can be put on hold. It's all right.
Situation/event	My thoughts and self-talk	Are these self-defeating or constructive?	If self-defeating, what would be constructive?
Situation/event	My thoughts and self-talk	Are these self-defeating or constructive?	If self-defeating, what would be constructive?

Challenging and dismantling errors in thinking

Errors in thinking consist of certain assumptions and ways of thinking that keep recurring, are habitual, and allow us to save time by not thinking constructively about events. They provide an easy response, but one that is neither time saving nor helpful. Errors in thinking 'save a penny and spend a pound,' because their consequences heavily tax our energy reserves, and generate high and unhealthy levels of stress or anxiety.

Errors in thinking need to be challenged and revised if we are to establish a constructive and healthy thought pattern.

EXAMPLES OF COMMON ERRORS IN THINKING

Assumptions	Challenge
All things are equally important and urgent.	Many things are not crucial or urgent. But they generate anxiety because I interpret them that way.
	Some things are crucial and/or urgent and cannot be left. Many things are not, and they can be postponed.
Getting uptight about unforeseen or unwanted events is inevitable.	If I'm stressed or anxious, what does a thing matter, unless it is truly crucial or urgent?
	Getting uptight is not inevitable or necessary, it is a habit. Lots of other people take these things pretty much in their stride.
	No, getting uptight often is mostly because I often interpret events in a self-defeating way.

Assumptions	Challenge
Everything has to go wrong. Life is against me succeeding.	Based on what evidence? What about people who, against all apparent odds, still succeed? Do I need to examine how I go about things – how I make decisions, and for what reasons? If I expect things to go wrong, isn't it highly likely I will contribute to that happening? Has 'life' really singled me out to be a victim?
People always let me down.	What real evidence supports this assumption? Are other people let down also? How does my experience compare with theirs? Have I on occasions let others down? Do I know anyone who always experiences other people as completely reliable? Do I automatically believe the best or the worst when people appear to let me down? Are my expectations reasonable?

Assumptions	Challenge
If I could go back in time: If I had… If only I did…	The benefit of hindsight is a fine thing. Of course I could be more knowledgeable, skilled and wise if I could have been then who I am now, or if I could go back as who I am now. How is this kind of thinking helpful? I was who I was. I made decisions and did things as the person I was, and was capable of being **then**. No amount of lamenting will change that. The only valid questions are perhaps: What can I learn from the past? What can I do differently now and in the future?
Everything has to be done perfectly or properly	No one could live up to that, without lying about the many occasions when they, quite rightly, didn't bother to do some things either perfectly or properly. Taking pride in doing important things well is admirable. But trying to do everything perfectly or properly is not necessary, important, reasonable, or admirable. It is plain unhealthy! Perhaps what is more needful is to be able to prioritise?

Other thinking habits:

Mind-reading: "She thinks I'm a failure;"
"They think I'm not as good as..."

Catastrophising: "Everything always turns out bad for me;"
"Things are always against me;"
"Now I will never be able to...;"
"No matter how hard I try everything always goes wrong."

Labelling: "I'm an idiot;" "I'm a failure;"
"I'm a lousy..." (Instead of "I did... poorly;" or
"I did not achieve...;" or
"I needed to...")

Over-generalising: Saying, "Always," "Never," "No-one," or "Everyone."

Fortune-telling: "Everyone is sure to...;" "I'm sure to mess it up;" "It's going to be a disaster;"
"I'm sure to feel dreadful when I..."

Rule-saying: "Should," "Must," or "Have to" (setting sometimes unrealistic expectations).

Black and white thinking: "Everything she does she gets right;"
"I've completely ruined everything;"
"He succeeds in everything... I never get it right!"

Examples you can think of:

....

....

....

....

....

STRUCTURED PROBLEM-SOLVING

For people who are anxious, it is common to feel threatened and overwhelmed by problems, and the thought of having to deal with them. So it can be really helpful to have a step-by-step methodical way of dealing with problems and making decisions. Through the method of structured problem-solving, it is possible to feel more in control of problems and to significantly reduce the feeling of being threatened or overwhelmed by them.

The **key elements** of this method include:

- Identifying and 'pinning down' the problems that have contributed to you feeling overwhelmed
- Thinking clearly and constructively about problems
- 'Taking stock' of how you've coped in the past: your personal strengths, and the support and resources available to you
- Providing a sound basis for important decision-making.

With this method you can work on a single problem or follow the process to tackle a number of problems.

Usually though – especially to begin with – it is best to deal with one problem that is specific and potentially solvable.

STRUCTURED PROBLEM-SOLVING INVOLVES 6 STEPS

Step 1
Write down the problem causing you worry or distress:

Step 2
Think about your options for dealing with this problem (try to think broadly – including good and not so good options); write them down:

1.	
2.	
3.	
4.	
5.	

Step 3

Write down the advantages and disadvantages of each option:

Step 4

Identify the best option(s) to deal with the problem:

1.	
2.	
3.	
4.	
5.	

Step 5 – List the steps needed to carry out each option (bear in mind the resources needed and pitfalls to overcome):

1. a.	
b.	
c.	
2. a.	
b.	
c.	
3. a.	
b.	
c.	
4. a.	
b.	
c.	
5. a.	
b.	
c.	

Step 6

Review your progress in carrying out your option(s):

What have I achieved? ....

....

What still needs to be done? ....

....

RESTORING A PATTERN OF NORMAL SLEEP

Sleep disturbance is common with anxiety – particularly the problem of not being able to get off to sleep at night. To achieve a pattern of normal sleep, it is important to practise sleep-promoting behaviours during the day, in the evening, at bedtime, and during the night.

Better Sleep Guidelines

During the day

- Organise your day. Regular times for eating meals, taking medicines, performing chores and other activities, help keep our inner clocks running smoothly.
- Regular exercise during the day (or early evening) can improve sleeping patterns.
- Set aside time for problem-solving and decision-making during the day to avoid worry or anxiety at night..
- Avoid napping during the day – go to bed and get up at regular times.

During the evening

- Put the day to rest. If you still have things on your mind, write them down or put them in your diary, to be dealt with tomorrow.
- Light exercise early in the evening may help sleep. Avoid exercise late in the evening, as this may make getting to sleep more difficult.
- Get into a routine of 'winding down' during the course of the evening, allowing at least half an hour of quiet activity, such as reading or listening to music, prior to bedtime.
- Avoid drinking caffeinated drinks after about 4pm, and don't drink more than 2 cups of caffeinated drinks each day (especially coffee, tea, cocoa and cola).
- Avoid smoking for at least an hour (preferably an hour and a half) before going to bed.
- Don't use alcohol to make you sleep and keep your intake moderate (limit yourself to 2 standard drinks each day). Have 1 or 2 alcohol-free days each week.

- Make sure your bed and bedroom are comfortable – not too cold or too warm.
- Ensure that your bedroom is dark and that the morning light does not filter in. However, if you have a tendency to oversleep, it may be helpful to let the morning light into the room.
- Avoid a heavy meal close to bedtime. If you are hungry, a light snack might help you get to sleep.

At bedtime

- Try to do the same things before you go to bed each night. Develop a calming bedtime routine, such as having a warm bath or shower, listening to relaxation music, or using a relaxation technique. This way your body will learn to know that (with these activities) you are getting ready to go to sleep.
- Go to bed when you feel 'sleepy tired' and not before.
- Don't watch TV or have conversations or arguments in bed. Keep your bed and bedroom only for sleep (and sexual activity).
- Turn the light off when you get into bed.
- Relax and tell yourself that sleep will come when it is ready. Enjoy relaxing your mind and body, even if you don't at first fall asleep.

During the night

- If you wake up too early in the night, don't lie awake for more than 30 minutes. Instead of just being awake or worrying, get out of bed and do something that is distracting yet relaxing. Return to bed only when you feel sleepy again.
- Get up at the same time each morning. Don't sleep late in the morning trying to make up for 'lost sleep.'
- If you live in a place or area where there are sounds or noises that might wake you from sleep, have earplugs handy to block out the noise.
- Avoid sleeping pills – they do not provide a long-term solution to sleep problems.

GRADUAL (GRADED) EXPOSURE

Anxiety resulting in avoidance and leaving

For people who are anxious, feeling noticeably or uncomfortably anxious in a particular situation can become associated with that or similar situations. Before long, they may begin to avoid these situations (for fear of becoming anxious) or, finding themselves in such situations, they may quickly leave (again, for fear of becoming anxious, or because they expected to be anxious, and that is what happened).

Unfortunately, both *avoidance and leaving* behaviours can make the problem of anxiety worse, because despite providing a feeling of relief and a drop in anxiety, these behaviours make it more and more difficult to face the situations that are feared. Two main problems arise with avoidance and leaving:

- Because it is not always possible to avoid feared situations, it can become very distressing when a person is forced to face them.
- Frequently avoiding feared situations, a person begins to tolerate less and less anxiety, avoiding an ever-widening number of potentially anxiety producing situations. This can become quite disabling, and significantly affect lifestyle and daily living.

Confronting fears through Gradual (graded) Exposure

A way of overcoming a fear of objects or situations that has proven to be successful in psychological therapy is confronting and facing fears using a method of *gradual or graded exposure.*

When things that are feared are confronted for long enough, fear eventually subsides, and the fear experienced in that situation next time around will be less. An important way of breaking the pattern of avoidance and leaving behaviour is by gradually confronting things that are feared, starting with easy situations and slowly building up the confidence and resilience to face the harder things. Part of, and essential to, this process of gradual exposure is remaining in the feared situation until there is a clearly experienced decrease in anxiety. It is also critical to success that the person experiencing anxiety use the controlled breathing technique and relaxation, prior to each occasion of gradual exposure, to limit their initial anxiety and to build their confidence in the achievability of each progressive step towards achieving their goal.

Controlled breathing can easily be practised while in the feared situation, as can relaxation, by noticing tension in particular muscles, and consciously tensing and relaxing them (as in the technique of Progressive Muscle Relaxation).

GRADUAL (GRADED) EXPOSURE

IMPORTANT

1. Use the controlled breathing and relaxation techniques to prepare for each step and to manage your anxiety in each feared situation.

2. List the situations that make you feel panicky or fearful:

   .... ☐
   .... ☐
   .... ☐
   .... ☐

3. Choose one of these situations (preferably the least feared) that you think you can cope with:

   ....
   ....

4.

Write down the specific fears you have about this situation:	If any of these fears are exaggerated, write down what you think is more likely to happen:

5. Plan a series of gradual steps for confronting/facing the feared situation, starting with small, not too threatening steps, progressing to more difficult ones:

Step 1

Step 2

Step 3

Step 4

Step 5

Step 6

Step 7

Step 8

REMEMBER

- *Just as anxiety rises initially when confronting a feared situation, it also subsides within a few minutes, but can last up to 75 minutes.*
- *When you put your first step into action, stay in the situation until your anxiety has lessened.*
- *Monitor your anxiety to see how it starts to decrease the longer you stay in the situation.*
- *Remain until you no longer feel anxious before ending the task.*

Practise this step until it no longer causes anxiety. Then (and only then) move on to the next step.

6. Put the first step into action.

7. Move through each step until you can manage the feared situation.

NOTE: You might keep a record of which steps work best for you in future use.

IMPORTANT

Exposure Therapy will not work if you are intoxicated or taking sedatives such as Valium or sleeping tablets.

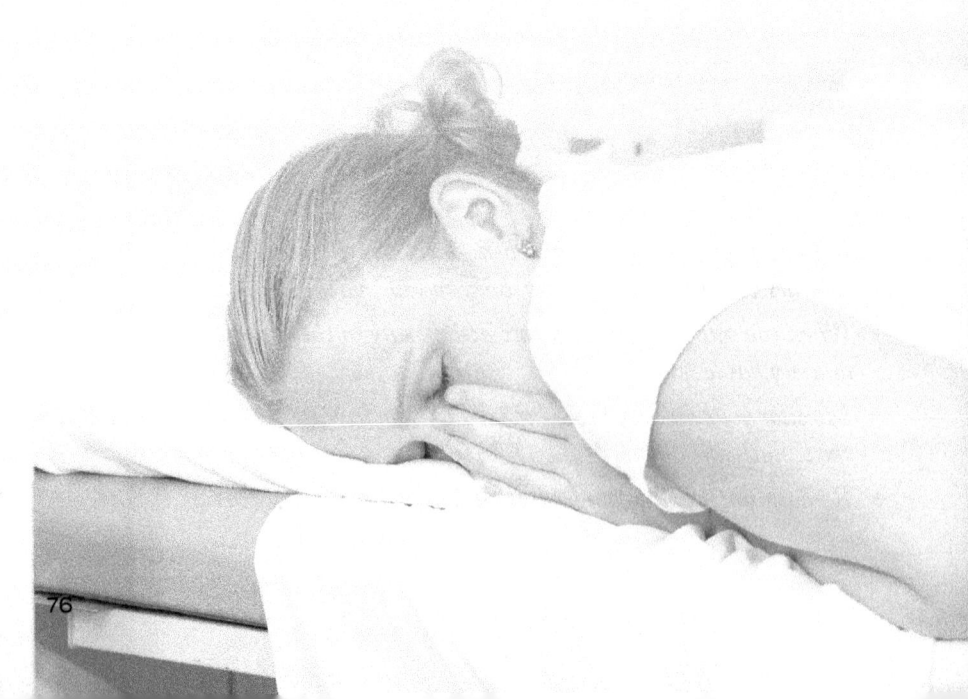

Tips for succeeding with Gradual (graded) Exposure

- Begin with an achievable step.
- Don't make your steps too easy or they will probably be unrewarding. Don't make your steps too hard or you will probably fail and become discouraged. Aim for regular and gradual progress.
- Move on to the next step only once the present step has been genuinely mastered. Since some steps are more difficult, at times progress may seem slow. Be patient with yourself and the process. Better to go slowly, than lose confidence and motivation by being abruptly set back by attempting too much.
- If the increase in difficulty of your steps turns out to be too high, put in some intermediate steps to make progress more manageable.
- Be prepared for setbacks. If a setback does occur, simply return to a previous step, and assess whether or not an intermediate step needs to be inserted. Don't be discouraged

  – setbacks do occur, because the whole process, no matter how well thought through, may need to be altered once actually 'put to the test.'
- Try to become conscious of your thoughts in approaching each step (particularly what you say to yourself in your head).

  – When you can identify exaggerated fears, try to replace them with more realistic thoughts about what is more likely to happen.

  – It can be helpful to write down your thoughts and 'self- talk' (preferably as soon as they occur), to challenge how rational they are.

Thoughts and self-talk	How exaggerated are these? How rational?	What would be a more rational and helpful way of thinking about the situation?

REDUCING ALCOHOL AND CAFFEINE CONSUMPTION

The problem with alcohol and anxiety

It is common for anxious people to 'settle the nerves' or to cover over their fears using alcohol. There are several problems with this:

- Alcohol becomes a substitute for developing confidence.
- Dependence can quickly (but often unknowingly) occur, with alcohol being used for anxiety control in more and more situations.
- Usual coping strategies (even if only partially effective) become neglected and even less effective when alcohol is used as a substitute.
- Alcohol can negatively affect the quality of sleep, and interferes with the effects of medication prescribed for anxiety.

Strategies for moderating alcohol consumption

- Try to avoid drinking at home alone – especially when you are feeling down or anxious.
- Try limiting your drinking to the evening meal time.
- Drink low-alcohol beers and mixes.
- Drink slowly (limit yourself to 2 standard drinks each day).
- Think ahead (and creatively) about how to avoid drinking excessively in situations (like the pub or social gatherings) where there is pressure to do so.
- Plan to have 2 alcohol-free days each week. Try to choose days when it is easiest to do so, like when an activity is planned for the evening that may be a useful distraction.
- Decide how much alcohol you will permit yourself to drink; measure it out, and only allow yourself that amount.
- Always try to stay within the **Australian Alcohol Guidelines**.

For Men and Women

Over a lifetime: If you drink no more than 2 standard drinks a day, you reduce the lifetime risk of harming yourself from alcohol-related disease or injury.

On a single occasion: Having no more than 4 standard drinks on a single occasion reduces the risk of alcohol-related injury arising from that occasion.

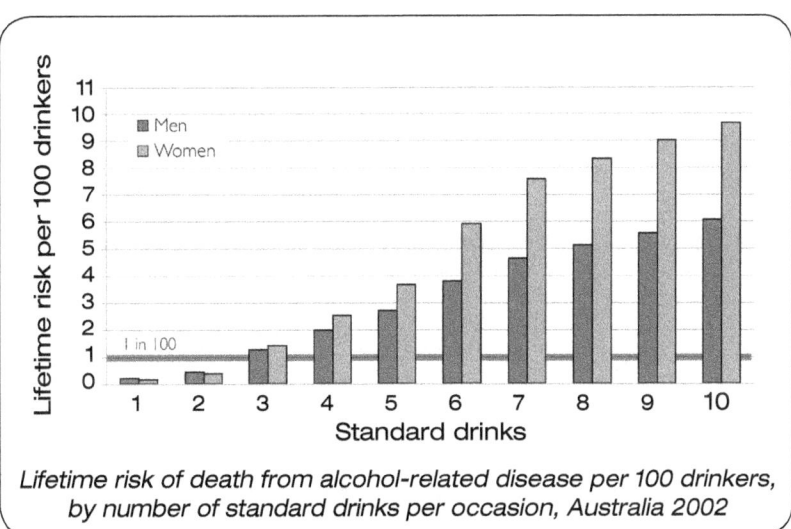

Lifetime risk of death from alcohol-related disease per 100 drinkers, by number of standard drinks per occasion, Australia 2002

For people who regularly drink 2 standard drinks per day, the lifetime risk of death from an alcohol-related disease is about 0.4 in 100 people with that drinking pattern. Above that level, the risk increases with the number of drinks per day, and is above 1 in 100 at 3 drinks per day. The risk increases more sharply for women than for men.

Source: National Health and Medical Research Council Australian Guidelines to Reduce Health Risks from Drinking Alcohol, Canberra: Commonwealth of Australia, 2009.

The problem with caffeine and anxiety

Caffeine is a substance that is derived from plants or is produced synthetically, and is an additive in a number of food products and over-the-counter medications such as pain relievers, appetite suppressants, and cold medicines. Most commonly, it is known to be an ingredient in tea, coffee, chocolate, cocoa, colas, and so called 'energy-boosting' beverages.

Tea and coffee are seen by most people merely as beverages, however they do contain caffeine.

Because caffeine is a central nervous system stimulant, in anxious people it can worsen symptoms of anxiety considerably. Consequently, it has been named in diagnoses such as *caffeine- related anxiety*, and *caffeine-related insomnia* (because of its adverse effect on sleep).

People with an anxiety problem would do well to eliminate caffeine from their diet – or at least reduce intake to a nominal amount. For tea and coffee drinkers, it is now possible to purchase these products in caffeine-reduced and decaffeinated forms. For people accustomed to a high caffeine intake, it is advisable to reduce consumption gradually to minimise potential withdrawal effects.

National Help/Information Lines

- Lifeline: 13 11 14
- Kids Help Line: 1800 55 1800
- Reconnexion: 1300 273 266
- SANE Australia: 1800 18 7263
- eheadspace: 1800 650 890 (for 12 to 25 year olds)
- healthdirect Australia: 1800 022 222
  (for health-specific assistance)

DISTURBING THOUGHTS

Disturbing thoughts are danger signs that should not be ignored.

Tick ☑ the signs that are familiar:

- ☐ Thinking things are hopeless and won't change in the future
- ☐ Thinking or saying to yourself:
  - life isn't worth living, or
  - people would be better off without me, or
  - nothing is ever going to get better, what's the point of going on, or
  - there will be no end to the mental/emotional pain I'm feeling, or
  - my relationship/marriage is in such trouble I just can't bear it; I don't want to go on….what's the point?
- ☐ Thoughts about death and dying, and how people would cope without you
- ☐ You have had thoughts about:
  - what you might do to yourself to end your life
  - when and where you would do it
  - what you might use to end your life
  - who you would put in your will, and the instructions you would leave for people, or the note you would write, for after your death.
- ☐ Thoughts about hurting others
- ☐ Thoughts about harming or mutilating yourself
- ☐ Being very suspicious about other people's intentions towards you
- ☐ Thoughts that you are being persecuted, taken advantage of or wronged in some way
- ☐ Being preoccupied with intrusive thoughts or perceptions that are important to you, but which others don't understand or accept the importance of.

Feelings that often accompany disturbing thoughts:

- ☐ Feeling an overwhelming sense of failure in life
- ☐ Feelings of emotional/mental pain that are almost unbearable and seem to get no better

- ☐ Feeling hopeless and helpless much of the time
- ☐ Feeling sad, miserable and/or depressed for days at a time
- ☐ Feeling unsafe

Behaviours that sometimes accompany disturbing thoughts:

- ☐ Becoming withdrawn, avoiding people and social events
- ☐ Increasing use of alcohol or other drugs to try to cover feelings of mental pain and hopelessness
- ☐ Becoming secretive about your thoughts and feelings of hopelessness and helplessness
- ☐ Being careless, taking needless risks, acting dangerously, or putting yourself in harm's way

Thoughts, feelings and behaviours of this kind need to be taken very seriously. **Do not ignore them.**

TAKE URGENT ACTION
Arrange to speak to a doctor OR phone

PHONE A 24-HOUR MENTAL HEALTH EMERGENCY LINE

National Help/Information Lines

Lifeline: 13 11 14
Suicide Call Back Service: 1300 659 467
Kids Helpline: 1800 55 1800
Australian Psychological Society Referral Line: 1800 333 497
SANE Australia: 1800 18 7263

State and Territory

ACT: Crisis Assessment and Treatment Team: 1800 629 354

NSW: Salvo Suicide Prevention & Crisis Line: Metro 02 9331 2000
Salvo Suicide Prevention & Crisis Line: Rural 1300 363 622
Suicide Prevention and Support: 1300 133 911
NSW Mental Health Line: 1800 011 511

NT: Mental Health on Call Team: Top End (08) 8999 4988
Mental Health on Call Team: Central Australia (08) 8951 7777

QLD: Salvo Crisis Counselling Service: Metro 07 3831 9016
Salvo Crisis Counselling Service: Rural 1300 363 622

SA: Mental Health Assessment and Crisis Intervention Service: 13 14 65

TAS: Mental Health Services Helpline: 1800 332 388

VIC: Mental Health Advice Line: 1300 280 737
SuicideLine: 1300 651 251

WA: Mental Health Emergency Response Line:
Metro 1300 555 788
Rural Link: Rural 1800 552 002
Samaritans Crisis Line: 1800 198 313

SOME THINGS TO CONSIDER IF YOU ARE EXPERIENCING SUICIDAL THOUGHTS

- No matter how bad your situation, no matter how overwhelming your mental/emotional pain, there is always a better option than considering suicide or self-harm – but it may not have occurred to you. Speak to a doctor (and other help can follow). Or phone a 24 hour Mental Health Crisis line.

- When people kill themselves, it seriously affects their family and friends. Feeling "They'd be better off without me" doesn't cancel out the fact that they would be greatly damaged – perhaps for life.

- Promise yourself (and someone else) that you will get help, that you will do it now, and you will not give up until you get it.

I promise, for my sake and for the sake of others, that I will get help NOW

Signed ....

- Suicidal thinking may be associated with depression but can also be associated with anxiety and distress.
- Break your silence and isolation: get help NOW.
- Feelings of hopelessness, helplessness, and overwhelming mental/emotional pain can be turned around with appropriate treatment.
- If you think a particular problem has brought you to this point, try using Structured Problem-Solving (included in this section). This may 'take some pressure off'. However, still speak to a doctor about your mental state.
- Who are the people who really matter to you? Think about why they do care, and the good things that have happened between you.
- If you have a gun, rope, pills, or anything else you've thought of using (or that is readily available) to kill yourself, either lock them up and give the key to someone for safe keeping, or hand them over to someone, so you are kept from harm's way until you have received help and are better.

Things can feel very different and look very different; energy, motivation, problem-solving ability, and hope for the future can be restored **if you act with courage** and speak to a doctor or phone a Mental Health Crisis Line.

More powerful than all problems is the courage to deal with them.

To help someone else
IMPORTANT

REMEMBER

- First and foremost recognise that you are not responsible for someone else's suicidal behaviour. You have no control over the person's will. If the person chooses to act in a self-harming or destructive way, he/she has chosen to do so; he/she is responsible.

- Asking a person if he/she has suicidal thoughts will not encourage the person to act on these thoughts, but will signal genuine concern and an avenue of hope.

- People who are experiencing suicidal thoughts, whether depressed or not, may not be easy to help. They may have become secretive and evasive, or may be so depressed or troubled that they view everything as pointless except ending how they feel. Persevere anyway.

Useful tips for helping someone who may be suicidal

- Think about the best way to approach the person – given what you know about his/her personality and temperament.

- Let the person know that you are seriously concerned.

    Suggest that he/she might see a doctor immediately or speak to a health professional recommended by a doctor
    – or ring a 24 hour Mental Health Crisis Line. Help the person to make the appointment or phone call. Offer to take or go with him/her to receive assistance.

- If you think the person won't listen to you, then consider who he/she usually confides in, feels comfortable with and/ or trusts. Maybe this nominated person could make the approach and encourage the person who may be depressed to seek assistance.

- Provide the person with a 24-hour crisis line number. Try to get the person to put the number where it won't be lost and will be accessible.

- Enlist the help of relatives or friends to keep a watchful eye on the person, to break his/her isolation, and to provide extra safety.

- Maybe you can help the person to work through a major problem rationally, resolve a relationship conflict, or get a new perspective on things.
- Encourage the person to think about what is valuable, worthwhile and precious in his/her life. As well, encourage the person to recognise who depends on and values him/her.
- Be as determined and resourceful as you can in finding a way to get the person to a doctor or appropriate health professional (or to seek help by phoning a Mental Health Crisis Line).
- Emphasise that mental/emotional pain, depression, low energy, and feelings of hopelessness and helplessness can be quickly turned around with appropriate treatment from a doctor. Left untreated, the person's mental state may deteriorate. The risk of acting on suicidal thoughts and feelings increases without treatment.
- Negotiate to take charge of any readily available means for acting on suicidal thoughts or impulses, such as guns, knives, rope, pills, car keys (if you think a vehicle might be used).
- Try to get agreement on a **No Harm/Seek Help promise** (an example is included below).
- Be determined, but respectful.
- Listen to the person carefully.
- Think safety.
- Avoid being overdramatic; be calm and thoughtful.
- Remind yourself that you are not responsible for someone else's suicidal behaviour.

NO HARM – SEEK HELP PROMISE

I give my word that I will not harm myself or put myself in danger and that I will seek help until I get help to deal with what is happening to me.

Signed: ....

Witnessed: .... **Dated:** ....

STRUCTURED PROBLEM-SOLVING

Some problems can feel absolutely overwhelming, and impossible to deal with.

Structured problem-solving is a method designed to help you feel in control of a problem, and to find a way through it.

The **key elements** of this method include:

- identifying and 'pinning down' the problems that have contributed to you feeling overwhelmed
- thinking clearly and constructively about problems
- 'taking stock' of how you've coped in the past: your personal strengths and the support and resources available to you
- providing a sound basis for important decision-making.

STRUCTURED PROBLEM-SOLVING INVOLVES 6 STEPS

Step 1
Write down the problem causing you worry or distress:

Step 2
Think about your options for dealing with this problem (try to think broadly – including good and not so good options); write them down:

Step 3

Write down the advantages and disadvantages of each option:

Step 4

Identify the best option(s) to deal with the problem:

Step 5 – List the steps needed to carry out each option (bear in mind the resources needed and pitfalls to overcome):

1. a.
b.
c.
2. a.
b.
c.
3. a.
b.
c.
4. a.
b.
c.
5. a.
b.
c.

Step 6

Review your progress in carrying out your option(s):

What have I achieved? ....

....

What still needs to be done? ....

....

SOME FACTS ABOUT SUICIDE

Though a significant number of people who die by suicide are affected by a mental health difficulty, and though depression is the most common mental health difficulty associated with suicide, many suicides appear not to be associated with mental ill-health.

Many who attempt to end their lives are not so much motivated by a desire for death, but to escape the emotional pain and psychological distress they are experiencing. This is important to understand, because when someone is on a path to suicide, it is often possible to intervene in a way that gives them the resources to cope with or overcome their pain and difficulties without resorting to self-harm.

Suicide is a major cause of death in Australia.

There were 2,864 deaths from intentional self-harm in 2014, resulting in a ranking as the 13th leading cause of all deaths. About three-quarters (75.4%) of people who died by suicide were male, making intentional self-harm the 10th leading cause of death for males. Deaths due to intentional self-harm occurred at a rate of 12.0 per 100,000 population in 2014.

While intentional self-harm accounts for a relatively small proportion (1.9%) of all deaths in Australia, it accounts for a greater proportion of deaths within specific age groups. For example, in 2014, over a quarter of deaths of males in each of the 15-19, 20-24, 25-29, and 30-34 year age groups were due to intentional self-harm (35.9%, 34.9%, 29.9% and 31.5%, respectively). Similarly for females, intentional self-harm deaths comprise a higher proportion of total deaths in younger age groups compared with older age groups (25.0% of deaths of persons aged 10-14 years, 27.1% of deaths of persons aged 15-19 years, 30.2% of deaths of persons aged 20-24 years and 20.4% of deaths in the 25-29 year age group).

Median age - The median age at death for intentional self-harm in 2014 was 44.4 years for males, 43.6 years for females and 44.2 years overall. In comparison, the median age for deaths from all causes in 2014 was 78.5 years for males, 84.8 years for females and 81.8 years overall.

Australian Bureau of Statistics (2014) Causes of Death, Australia, Intentional Self Harm 2014, (3303.0), Canberra, ABS

Factors that contribute to suicide risk

- Marital breakdown/relationship problems
- Bereavement
- Depression (or other mental health difficulties)
- Unemployment
- Financial problems – including a sudden change in financial circumstances
- Previous suicide attempt
- High levels of stress, distress and depleted ('run down') emotional and personal coping resources
- Ready access to a firearm, pills, or other means of committing suicide
- Alcohol dependence and/or abuse
- Deliberate self-harm
- Isolation

Factors believed to diminish suicide risk

- Family connectedness
- Responsibility for children and others
- Close relationships/friendships
- Employment
- A sense of meaning and purpose in life
- Personal resilience and problem-solving skills
- Being connected to a community and social activities
- Good mental health
- A preparedness to seek out early help for mental health difficulties
- A belief that suicide is wrong
- Lack of access to guns

Major issues for men

Some of the most telling issues linked with male suicide in Australia include:
- unemployment and/or financial problems
- alcohol use, marijuana or other drug dependence
- experiencing a sense of powerlessness
- a sense of failure in life, towards family, and financially
- family/relationship problems
- loneliness, isolation
- physical or mental health difficulties
- unaddressed depression.

Most telling issues relative to age:
- unemployment for men of employable age
- a sense of failure appears most significant to men under 45 years of age.
- family/relationship problems and a sense of failure appear to be significant factors for men aged 45-49 years.
- physical and/or mental health difficulty and family problems appear to be significant factors for men aged 60-69 years.
- loneliness or physical illness appear to be significant for men aged 70 years.

DISTURBING THOUGHTS

WARNING SIGNS OF A PROBLEM WITH INSOMNIA

Tick ☑ the signs that are familiar

- ❑ Difficulty falling asleep
- ❑ Difficulty staying asleep
- ❑ Waking up too early at the end of the sleep period
- ❑ Difficulty getting back to sleep after waking
- ❑ Feeling worried, annoyed, frustrated, anxious, or angry at bedtime or while lying in bed trying to go to sleep
- ❑ Racing thoughts when trying to go to sleep or when waking in the night
- ❑ Feeling physically or mentally tired during the day
- ❑ Your sleep has been disturbed for 3 or more days per week for at least a month
- ❑ Sleep disturbance is causing you significant personal distress or interferes with your social life or ability to work
- ❑ Poor quality of sleep (not waking feeling refreshed despite having been asleep for a reasonable period of time)
- ❑ You're very concerned about your lack of sleep (most of the time), and the consequences of this lack of sleep
- ❑ Spending excessive time in bed and experiencing sleep broken by frequent awakenings
- ❑ Falling asleep early each evening (before 9pm), waking very early and being unable to return to sleep

If some of these signs are familiar and poor sleep is affecting your life:

TAKE ACTION
Arrange to speak to a doctor

Why speak to a doctor?

Restoring a normal pattern of sleep usually requires little more than the use of some simple guidelines and strategies. But because there are many factors that can cause or contribute to insomnia, requiring medical diagnosis, treatment, or referral, it is important to speak to a doctor. These include:

- medical disorders associated with insomnia
- mental health difficulties associated with insomnia
- prescription medications
- use of non-prescription drugs and alcohol
- sleep difficulties associated with malfunctioning body organs.

ABOUT INSOMNIA

Sleep difficulties are one of the most common complaints people make when presenting to doctors in general practice.

Twenty to twenty-five per cent of Australians report suffering from some form of lasting insomnia at some time in their lives. Up to 12% have long-term (chronic) difficulty either going to sleep or maintaining sleep.

Common complaints of people with insomnia are:

- difficulty falling asleep
- difficulty staying asleep
- waking up early at the end of the sleep period
- feeling anxious, irritable, worried or depressed – especially at bedtime
- racing thoughts when waiting to go to sleep or when waking up in the night
- feeling physically or mentally tired during the day.

What are the effects of insomnia?

Sleep is a natural process that allows the body and brain time to recover from daily activity. During sleep, the body makes chemicals which help it grow and repair, and the immune system becomes more active to fight infection and illness.

Sleep is also important for emotional balance and a healthy mood state. It is also thought that sleep is a time when memories, experiences, and skills are sorted and stored. But what about when sleep is disturbed, when people fail to get enough sleep, or their quality of sleep is poor?

Some of the consequences of insomnia

- Fatigue (due to tiredness) is involved in approximately 1 in 6 fatal road accidents in Australia.
- An older person with insomnia has 4 times the risk of having a fall and suffering a major injury.
- Tiredness and fatigue are responsible for 52.5% of work-related accidents and almost 29% of accidents around the home. Nearly 10% of people with chronic insomnia experience serious accident or injury.
- Staying awake for 17 hours decreases performance, the same as a blood alcohol level of 0.05%.
- After 5 nights of poor sleep, 3 drinks have the same effect on the body as 6 would when the person is well rested.
- People experiencing insomnia are 25% more likely to miss work.
- Studies of people with insomnia show that it impairs concentration, memory, and the ability to accomplish daily tasks, and affects interpersonal relationships.

What causes insomnia?

Insomnia commonly begins during times of increased life stress. Most people at some stage in their lives experience sleeplessness due to lying awake at night thinking about personal problems, work, or their finances. This sleep difficulty is only a temporary problem that will likely resolve within a few days or weeks. Sometimes though, especially if the stressful issue is major and a person's ability to function is significantly affected by sleeplessness, he/she will *also* become preoccupied with the inability to get to sleep. The effect is a vicious cycle of anxiety and worry about not sleeping, feeding into and worsening the problem of sleeplessness itself. In this way, a temporary problem of sleeplessness can develop into insomnia.

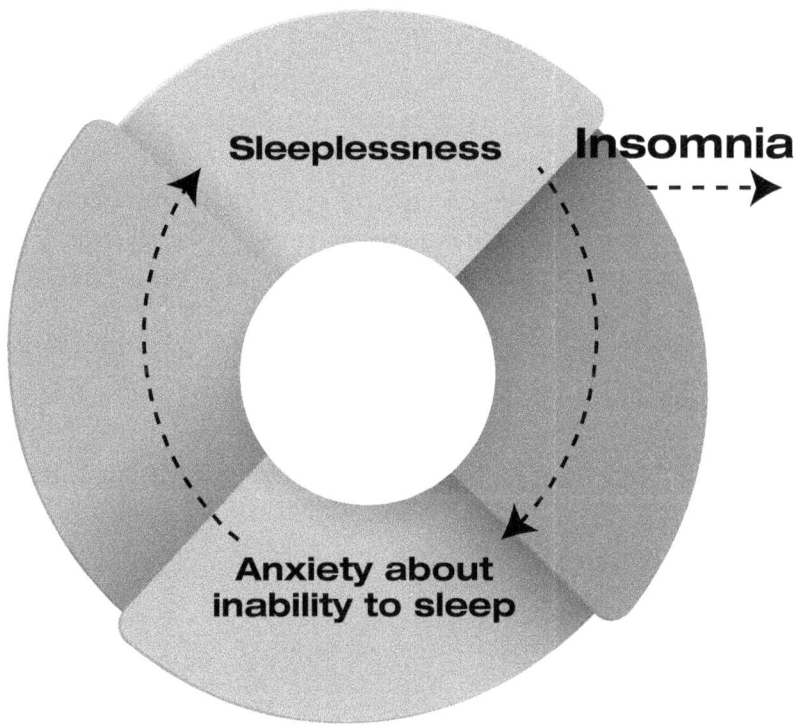

Though times of increased stress are a common beginning for insomnia, there are actually many factors that can cause or contribute to it such as:
- ageing
- lifestyle commitments
- physical disorders
- mental disorders
- prescription medication
- non-prescription drugs and alcohol
- use of bright screen electronic devices (iPad, smartphone, tablet, computer) late in the evenings.

What about using medication?

Medication may be prescribed for a short period of time (3 to 5 days). However, the preferred approach to overcome sleep difficulties is NOT to use medication.

The use of sleeping pills (sedative hypnotics) for any length of time can cause more problems than it solves: dependence, addiction, returning symptoms, side-effects and for older people in particular, an increased risk of falls.

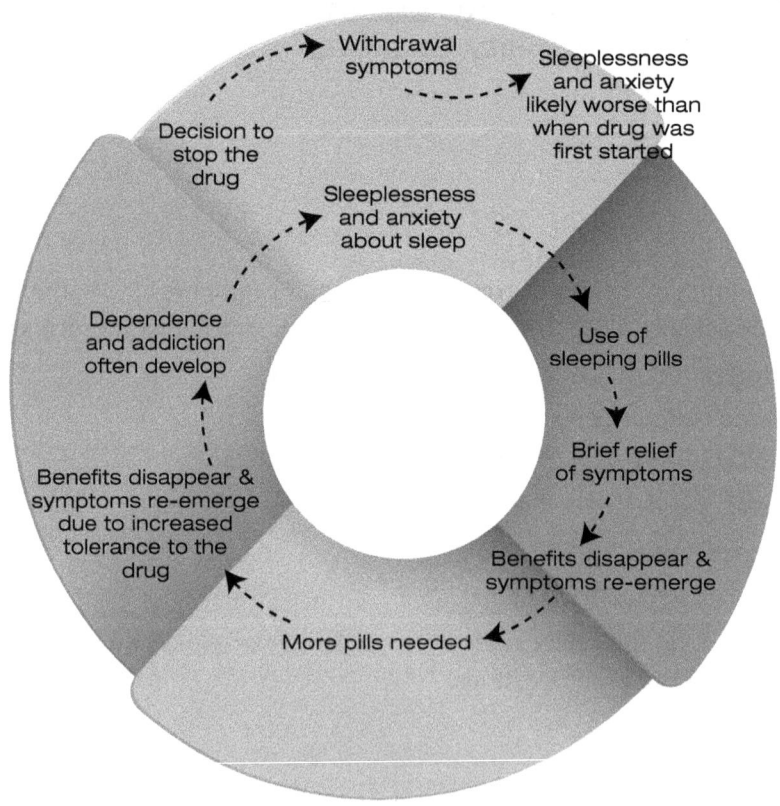

PROBLEMS ASSOCIATED WITH SLEEP MEDICATION

SELF-HELP SLEEP GUIDELINES AND THERAPIES

Individual differences in the need for sleep

People differ in the amount of sleep they need. Some people appear to need 9 to 10 hours sleep each night, whereas others can wake refreshed and function well during the day on 4 to 5 hours sleep each night. As people get older, they generally require less sleep. Few people in their sixties need as much sleep as when they were in their thirties. Teenagers tend to need as much sleep as small children – around 10 hours per night.

You are the best person to judge whether you have a problem with sleep. You may feel fine and function well even though you don't get a lot of sleep. However, if this is not the case, and your life is being adversely affected by insomnia, there are some very effective measures you can take to establish a better pattern of sleep.

Better Sleep Guidelines

To establish a better pattern of sleep, often all that is necessary is to practise sleep promoting behaviours during the day, in the evening, at bedtime, and during the night.

During the day

- Organise your day. Regular times for eating meals, taking medicines, performing chores and other activities, help keep our inner clocks running smoothly.
- Regular exercise during the day (or early evening) can improve sleeping patterns.
- Set aside time for problem-solving and decision-making during the day to avoid worry or anxiety at night..
- Avoid napping during the day – go to bed and get up at regular times.

During the evening

- Put the day to rest. If you still have things on your mind, write them down or put them in your diary, to be dealt with tomorrow.
- Light exercise early in the evening may help sleep. Avoid exercise late in the evening, as this may make getting to sleep more difficult.
- Get into a routine of 'winding down' during the course of the evening, allowing at least half an hour of quiet activity, such as reading or listening to music, prior to bedtime.
- Avoid drinking caffeinated drinks after about 4pm, and don't drink more than 2 cups of caffeinated drinks each day (especially coffee, tea, cocoa and cola).
- Avoid smoking for at least an hour (preferably an hour and a half) before going to bed.
- Don't use alcohol to make you sleep and keep your intake moderate (limit yourself to 2 standard drinks each day). Have 1 or 2 alcohol-free days each week.
- Make sure your bed and bedroom are comfortable – not too cold or too warm.
- Ensure that your bedroom is dark and that the morning light does not filter in. However, if you have a tendency to oversleep, it may be helpful to let the morning light into the room.
- Avoid a heavy meal close to bedtime. If you are hungry, a light snack might help you get to sleep.

At bedtime

- Try to do the same things before you go to bed each night.
  Develop a calming bedtime routine, such as having a warm bath or shower, listening to relaxation music, or using a relaxation technique. This way your body will learn to know that (with these activities) you are getting ready to go to sleep.
- Go to bed when you feel 'sleepy tired' and not before.
- Don't watch TV or have conversations or arguments in bed. Keep your bed and bedroom only for sleep (and sexual activity).
- Turn the light off when you get into bed.
- Relax and tell yourself that sleep will come when it is ready. Enjoy relaxing your mind and body, even if you don't at first fall asleep.

During the night
- If you wake up too early in the night, don't lie awake for more than 30 minutes. Instead of just being awake or worrying, get out of bed and do something that is distracting yet relaxing. Return to bed only when you feel sleepy again.
- Get up at the same time each morning. Don't sleep late in the morning trying to make up for 'lost sleep.'
- If you live in a place or area where there are sounds or noises that might wake you from sleep, have earplugs handy to block out the noise.
- Avoid sleeping pills – they do not provide a long-term solution to sleep problems.

Taking note of your sleep pattern

Before looking at the role or relevance of self-help sleep therapies, it is best to be clear about the factors or patterns evident in your sleep over a 2 week period. There may be some features of your sleep difficulty of which you are unaware.

You may be able to simply recall enough of this information to complete a sleep diary. If not, then monitor what happens for the next 2 weeks. A solution cannot be matched to a problem until the problem is clearly defined.

Sleep Diary

DAY	Time of getting to bed	Time taken to fall asleep	No. of times woke up	Time spent awake during night

Time of waking up in morning	Time of getting up	Daytime naps	Exercise (type & duration)	Alcohol, caffeine, drugs	Significant events today

CHOOSING A SELF-HELP THERAPY

Sleep Pattern	Sleep Therapy
Insomnia is affecting your ability to enjoy life. You worry about not sleeping or how you'll cope the next day.	Better Sleep Guidelines should suffice
You don't seem to be able to relax in bed. Your mind races, you feel tense, you toss and turn a lot.	Relaxation Therapy
Going to bed has become associated with not sleeping. You get worried, anxious and frustrated. You feel less sleepy after turning out the lights than before you went to bed.	Stimulus Control Therapy

CHOOSING A SELF-HELP THERAPY

Sleep Pattern	Sleep Therapy
You have been spending an excessive amount of time in bed (9 or more hours). You do this in the hope of trying to catch up on lost sleep.	Bedtime Restriction Therapy
You don't get to sleep until the early hours of the morning. You have difficulty getting up early each morning even with an alarm.	Bright Light Therapy (Morning)
You tend to fall asleep before 9pm each night. You wake too early and can't get back to sleep.	Bright Light Therapy (Evening)

RELAXATION THERAPY

There are many different relaxation methods including: meditation, self-hypnosis, mental imagery, yoga, special relaxation music. These (and many others) are readily available from book stores, libraries, and on the internet.

Progressive Muscle Relaxation

- You will need about 15 minutes for this relaxation exercise.
- Find a quiet place where you won't be interrupted.
- Sit in a comfortable straight-backed chair, with your feet flat on the floor.
- Close your eyes and use the controlled breathing technique for about 5 minutes.
- Tense each of the following muscle groups for 5 seconds, then relax them completely for 15-20 seconds (pay particular attention to the different sensations of tension and relaxation):
    1. Curl both your fists and tighten your biceps and forearms (as if lifting weights). Relax.
    2. Wrinkle up your forehead; tighten the muscles in your face causing your face to wrinkle; purse your lips and press your tongue against the roof of your mouth; hunch your shoulders. Relax.
    3. Arch your back as you take a deep breath into your chest. Relax.
    4. Taking a deep breath, gently push out your stomach. Relax.
    5. Pull your feet and toes backwards tightening your shins. Relax.
    6. Curl your toes at the same time as tightening your calves, thighs and buttocks. Relax.
- Close your eyes and use the controlled breathing technique for about 5 minutes.
- Now resume normal activities in a calm and peaceful manner.

Tips and cautions on the use of progressive muscle relaxation

- Be patient with yourself and this technique. You may only experience partial success at first. In time, it should be possible for you to relax your whole body quickly and successfully. Practise is the key.
- Be careful when you are tensing your neck and back. Don't tighten your muscles beyond what feels comfortable for you.
- To achieve the best results with this technique it's important to let go of the tension in a group of muscles you have tensed instantly. Releasing tension slowly may seem to relax muscles, when in fact it may just sustain tension. When you release muscle tension, do it instantly and let the muscles suddenly become limp.

Stimulus Control Therapy

Not being able to get to sleep may be because a negative association or link has developed between going to bed and not being able to sleep. It may be that the original reason for not being able to sleep (for example, a stressful event) has resolved, but difficulty getting to sleep continues.

Your bedtime routine, your bed and bedroom, even turning out the light, may have become the stimulus – the thing that triggers (psychologically) a negative reaction of anxiety, frustration, or worry. So the process of going to bed sets off a reaction that prevents you getting to sleep. This is called conditioned insomnia.

To turn this around, what is needed is to make your bed and bedroom a positive (rather than a negative) trigger for sleep.

Here is what to do:

Step 1 Only use your bedroom for sleep or sexual activity (no eating, smoking, TV, arguing, reading).

Step 2 Get up and out of bed at the same time each morning. Do this even on weekends or if you have had a late night.

Step 3 Don't go to bed at night until you feel sleepy.

Step 4 When you have gone to bed and turned the light out, if you don't get to sleep within about 15 minutes, get up again and do something distracting but relaxing. When you feel sleepy go back to bed. Don't try too hard to fall asleep; just relax.

Step 5 If you can't get to sleep quickly, repeat step 4. Repeat this step as often as necessary until you can fall asleep quickly.

Step 6 Resist napping during the day, even after a night of poor sleep.

Step 7 Follow these steps for several weeks, until a better pattern of sleep is established.

IMPORTANT

- Following the steps of Stimulus Control Therapy may take perseverance, and may result in less sleep than usual in the first few days. However, the build-up of tiredness that will likely result, will eventually help you fall asleep more quickly. After a while a new positive association between bed, bedroom, bedtime routine, and sleep will be established, so that these things trigger sleep rather than anxious wakefulness.

Bedtime Restriction Therapy

People who have a problem with insomnia can end up spending more and more time in bed in an attempt to catch up on lost sleep. This actually makes the problem worse:

- Negative feelings can become associated with being in bed. Such feelings increase alertness, making it more difficult to fall back to sleep when waking in the night; which in turn can cause daytime exhaustion, which likely occurs because of the constant physical tension brought about by sleep anxiety.
- Sleep spread across such a long time in bed becomes shallow and fragmented.

The principle behind Bedtime Restriction Therapy is to significantly decrease the time spent in bed and to consolidate sleep into that time. This helps to improve sleep quality and a person's sense of control over sleep. Put another way, this therapy aims to decrease shallow unrefreshing sleep, and increase (within a much shorter sleep period) the amount of deep, quality, refreshing sleep. The effect should also be to diminish sleep anxiety and night time awakening, and increase daytime energy.

Here is what to do:

Step 1 Use the Sleep Diary (included in this section) to record your total daily sleep time over 2 weeks.

Step 2 Excluding the times you spent lying awake in bed, calculate the average amount of sleep you've had each night.

Step 3 Choose a wake-up time that suits your personal circumstances and stick to it every day of the week.

Step 4 Now, set a regular bedtime. Simply calculate back from your set wake-up time by the average number of hours of nightly sleep you've been getting. For example if you've been getting 5 hours of sleep each night, and you've set your wake-up time at 6.30am, then your regular bedtime will need to be set at 1.30am.

Step 5 After a few nights, if you have fallen asleep sooner and have slept better than before, increase your bedtime by 30 minutes – which means going to bed 30 minutes earlier. If you find you are awake for more than 40 minutes each night (including the time it takes to get to sleep and time spent awake in the night) do not extend your time in bed.

Step 6 After a few more nights, if you are still falling asleep easily and remaining asleep, increase your bedtime by a further 30 minutes.

Step 7 Repeat step 6 until you get to the point of no longer falling asleep quickly, and no longer sleeping well through the night (i.e. when your total being-awake time exceeds 40 minutes). At this point you are spending too long in bed, and need to reduce it by 30 minutes to the previous bedtime.

IMPORTANT
- Once you have worked out your ideal bedtime, stick to it.
- At first, you will probably feel quite tired and maybe even irritable until you adapt to a new and much shorter sleep schedule.
- If you feel sleepier than usual when you wake up in the morning, or during the day, don't be tempted to nap. Make yourself persevere, because some pressure of insufficient sleep early in this process will help your improvement.

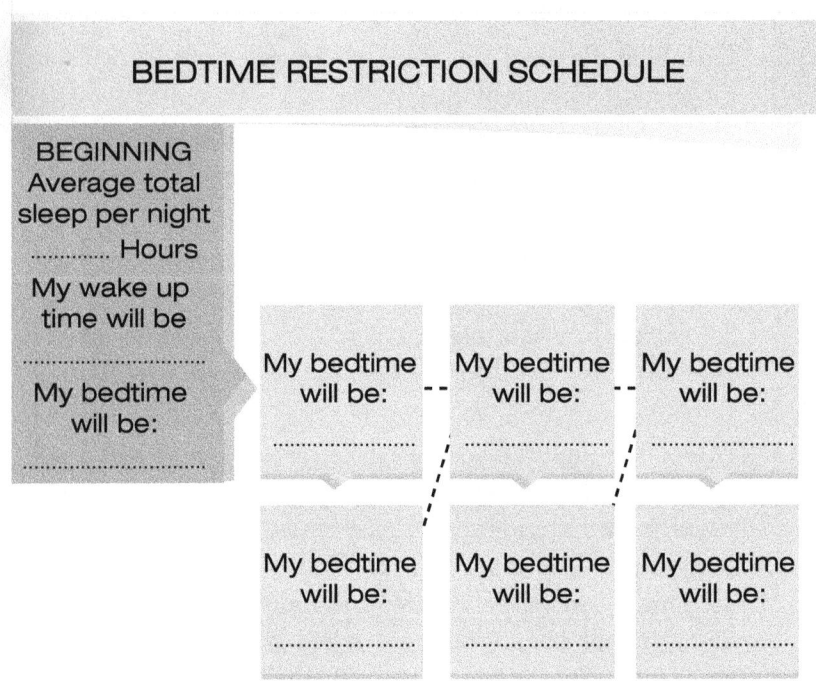

Bright Light Therapy – Morning

Research has found that feeling sleepy and the desire to sleep is associated with the production and release of a hormone called melatonin, which then leads to a decrease in body temperature. The release of melatonin (and change in body temperature) is usually synchronised with the pattern of sleep at night, and being awake and alert during the day. However if, for example, you do not fall asleep until 2am, and then find it hard to wake up until 9am, the release of melatonin for sleep is occurring too late in the evening.

This problem with *delayed* sleep is especially common among young people, who tend to sleep in until late in the day when they don't have to get up – like on weekends.

Our biological clock is influenced by the cycle of light and darkness (night and day). Light (through our eyes) stimulates a location in the brain that governs the release of melatonin.

More exposure to light early in the morning (between 6am and 9am) results in melatonin levels quickly dropping and the body temperature rising. This in turn can begin to alter the time when melatonin is released (and the body temperature drops) in the evening: it will occur earlier, readying the body for sleep. In this way, Bright Light Therapy early in the morning can help you feel sleepy earlier in the evening. It can help synchronise the day and night cycle with the melatonin and body temperature cycle.

Here is what to do:

Step 1   Keep to a regular wake-up time every day – including on weekends.

Step 2   Expose your vision to bright light between 6am and 9am. 20 minutes of exposure on a bright sunny day may be enough, but if there is cloud cover, or if it is a dull day, 30 to 60 minutes will be needed.

Never look directly at the sun; instead look into a sunlit environment or the sky. Do not wear sunglasses.

It may be easiest to accomplish bright light exposure through a daily routine of morning walking, gardening, or some other outdoor activity.

Step 3   Avoid bright light in the evening so that your body gets the clear message that it is not daytime.

Though Bright Light Therapy (morning) should improve your sleep pattern within a few days, you will probably need to keep it up for about a month to establish your new sleep-wake cycle. If you experience relapse, then simply recommence the therapy.

Bright Light Therapy — Evening

The tendency to fall asleep too early in the evening (before 9pm) and then waking very early and not being able to get back to sleep, is a common problem for older people (who are undergoing changes in their body temperature cycle), shift workers, and people experiencing a prolonged illness. Jet lag may be another factor associated with the problem of an *advanced sleep pattern*.

The principle of Bright Light Therapy in the evening is that it sends a message to the brain to delay the release of melatonin and a decrease in body temperature until later in the evening. This also has the effect of delaying the final wake-up time, so that early morning awakenings become less frequent.

Here is what to do:

Step 1   Spend 30 to 60 minutes outdoors late in the day or early evening. If there is cloud cover you may need at least 60 minutes outdoors. In winter, you may need to speak to your doctor about obtaining a Light Box. Artificial light exposure between 8pm and 10pm has been found to be effective. Other indoor bright lights (like a desk lamp) may also be of some value.

Step 2   Avoid morning sunlight and other bright light within one to two hours after waking.

Step 3   Get light exercise early in the evening (20 to 30 minutes).

This raises body temperature, lowers melatonin, and can improve sleep four to six hours later. Avoid strenuous exercise early in the morning.

An improvement in sleep pattern should occur within a few days. Therapy should continue for a month. If relapse occurs it can be recommenced.

For older people, general evening light exposure may need to become an ongoing part of their lifestyle.

*Adapted from: **Insomnia Management**. (Adelaide, Department of Human Services: Environment Health Branch, 2000).*

Structured Problem-Solving

Worrying about problems before bed can make it very difficult to get to sleep. That is why it is best to set aside time for problem-solving during the day.

Structured problem-solving is a method designed to help you feel in control of a problem, and to find a way through it. Even if a problem can't be fully solved during the day, at least having used a documented method you will have made a start, and have less cause to feel anxious and out of control at the end of the day or at bedtime.

The **key elements** of this method include:

- identifying and 'pinning down' the problems that have contributed to you feeling overwhelmed
- thinking clearly and constructively about problems
- 'taking stock' of how you've coped in the past: your personal strengths and the support and resources available to you
- providing a sound basis for important decision-making.

STRUCTURED PROBLEM-SOLVING INVOLVES 6 STEPS

Step 1
Write down the problem causing you worry or distress:

Step 2
Think about your options for dealing with this problem (try to think broadly – including good and not so good options); write them down:

Step 3
Write down the advantages and disadvantages of each option:

Step 4
Identify the best option(s) to deal with the problem:

Step 5

List the steps needed to carry out each option (bear in mind the resources needed and pitfalls to overcome):

a.	b.
c.	d.

Step 6

Review your progress in carrying out your option(s):

What have I achieved? ....

....

What still needs to be done? ....

....

INSOMNIA

CONFLICT

Conflict happens when we discover we disagree with another person about something – which can be a useful discovery if we make an effort to handle it in the right way. It often carries with it some strong feelings, which have the potential to either fuel a process of problem-solving, negotiation, and resolution – or more heated conflict into all out war!

Conflict that is quite minor may not need any kind of thoughtful process to resolve it. A little time may suffice; although how you feel about it and how your partner, friend or colleague feels may vary.

Even with the best intentions, not all conflict can be resolved immediately. Accepting change in a relationship – new ideas, different ways of thinking and going about things – may need some time for adjustment.

IMPORTANT

- A healthy relationship is an evolving, changing relationship. It is flexible and able to adapt to changing needs, beliefs, values, ideas, and circumstances.
- Conflict is an inevitable and unavoidable part of a healthy relationship. That's why knowing how to work with conflict is so important.

The Potential of Conflict

Positive Potential

Dealt with well, conflict can have some quite positive outcomes for a relationship:

- People can get to know each other better: what they think, how they feel, and what is important to them.
- Energy is released that can break through obstacles to make necessary change and improvement occur.
- It can clarify and 'clear up' false beliefs, misconceptions and false assumptions.
- It can disperse tension and stress, and bring relief and relaxation.
- It can help a relationship evolve, move forward, and strengthen.

Negative Potential

Conflict that is dealt with poorly can have quite negative consequences for a relationship:

- Conflict that is prolonged and not properly 'worked with' can be very damaging for both people and the relationship.
- Avoiding conflict can cause anger and resentment to build up and explode, causing damage hugely disproportional to the issue that caused the conflict in the first place.
- Suppression of conflict prevents opportunities for individuals to make the changes and adjustments necessary in a relationship, and to stay 'connected,' when faced with the inevitable emergence of differences and different needs.
- To ignore conflict is to ignore and devalue the very differences that may have attracted 2 people to each other, and that give the relationship energy and variety.
- The more poorly conflict is handled, the more trivial will be the things that trigger it and the more habitual conflict will likely become.
- Conflict left unresolved can cause growing confusion, exaggeration, and feelings of powerlessness, helplessness, and despair – ingredients that can contribute to the development of anxiety or depression.

WORKING WITH CONFLICT

Working with conflict means *resolving* conflict by using it to achieve a positive outcome, or at least an outcome that is better than continuing conflict.

There are a number of 'tools' and guidelines that are generally needed for this task:

You need to have the will

You have to be genuine about having the will to resolve conflict. Are you prepared to make concessions and do the work, or do you really just want to vent anger or resentment? You will need to say how you feel, but that is quite different to launching a personal attack, blaming, or accusing – all of which are counter-productive.

'Set the stage' for working with conflict

- If you have the energy and you are calm enough (if not, delay), identify, acknowledge, say what the conflict is in your view, and allow the other person to express his/her view (without interrupting or being 'hooked' into an argument).
- Decide that for your part you will remain calm and respectful (even if the other person doesn't).
- Decide that you won't make things worse by using put-downs, making nasty remarks, accusing, blaming, screaming, shouting or threatening, or by being loud or overbearing.
- Decide that you won't try to get your own way by using tears, false information, aggression, anger, or manipulation (like using guilt or mind games).
- Acknowledge the emotion that the other person is feeling around the conflict.
- Ask the other person if he/she would be prepared to help work out a solution with you or a way of resolving your difference.
- Say how you feel about the issue without elaborating, blaming, insinuating, or accusing. Your feelings are valid but, if you take them out on the other person, chances are he/she will become angry and you will lose the opportunity to discuss the issue.
- Having both acknowledged the conflict, and having agreed to work it out, decide together when you will do so.

Now may not be a good time, because of high emotion, too little energy, or the time, place or circumstances are inappropriate.

Explore and define the problem

- It is crucial to effective conflict resolution to clearly define the problem together. There are several things to consider here:
    - In defining the problem (and issues), don't 'rope in' other issues and feelings that don't belong; these are probably best dealt with at another time.
    - Listen to each other patiently and without interruption.

Make a *real* effort to understand the other person's point of view: Try to imagine yourself in his/her position. Be courteous, give the person your full attention (rather than rehearsing what you are going to say, in your mind), and allow him/her at least equal time to speak.

- Be really honest and open about what you might have done to make the conflict or disagreement worse. Don't demand or expect the same concession from the other person.

- Avoid any criticism of the other person's view and don't discount his/her feelings. Should it be the case that the other person is rigid in his/her view, criticism may merely serve to reinforce the person's rigidity. Freedom from criticism and pressure leaves open the possibility of a 'change of heart.'

Find a Solution

This is the part of the process for resolving conflict that can require **courage** (to accept change), **humility** (being prepared to make concessions), **empathy** (appreciating their point of view and experience), and **forgiveness** (being prepared to 'bury the hatchet,' and truly relinquish any ill-feeling, to allow for a fresh start).

Do some brainstorming: think of a range of ways in which your disagreement or conflict could be resolved:

- What do you both need or want?
- How would things need to be different for you both to feel comfortable?
- What would need to change?
- What compromise or concessions are you both prepared to accept?

Remember to remain calm, patient, and respectful.

- Conflict resolution works only when you don't need, or insist on gaining, the upper hand – which just makes the other person the loser. Some immediate compromise may be necessary. In time, one or both of you may feel differently and have a change of heart – away from the more definite position currently held. Sometimes, being prepared to compromise a little can go a long way to cooling down the conflict and any likelihood of it continuing.

- Conflict resolution is about working together to find a solution that doesn't leave either of you feeling cheated or the loser. If you win, the chances are, you have lost. The problem will merely have been obscured, and the other person's feelings overridden. Both will likely return with a vengeance!
- The real value of any solution is that it can pass the test of these questions:

    – Does this solution leave us both sufficiently satisfied not to want to harbour anger, resentment, annoyance or ill will, from now on?

    – Does this solution leave me feeling heard, respected, and valued?

    – Does this solution allow me to be true to myself and my needs?

Carry out the solution

- Write down what you have both agreed to work on, do, or change.
- Carry out the solution.
- If something happens that means you can't keep up your part of the agreement, discuss this openly and honestly with the other person, and renegotiate an agreeable alternative.
- If a solution doesn't look like it's going to work, invite the other person to work with you on finding a new one.

Agree on a date for review

- Agree on a date to review how well the solution has worked or is working.
- If there is a problem, you can work together to solve it before conflict occurs again.

What to do if things can't be worked out

Sometimes, with the best will in the world, it just doesn't seem possible to resolve a conflict ourselves – perhaps because feelings are too strong, or the issues are very difficult or complicated. A third person from outside the situation can be very helpful in providing some objectivity, assisting us to think more broadly and creatively, and perhaps to make better sense of what we want, mean, feel, and can reasonably expect of each other.

Because conflict resolution requires time, energy, honesty, and vulnerability, it pays to try to find the right person to help you 'first time around' rather than having to go over the matter again with someone else.

Speak to your doctor, or contact a health professional to have someone recommended to you. (Obviously, you will need to discuss this with, and gain the agreement of, the person with whom you are in conflict.) It is rarely the case that conflict can't be resolved with some competent assistance.

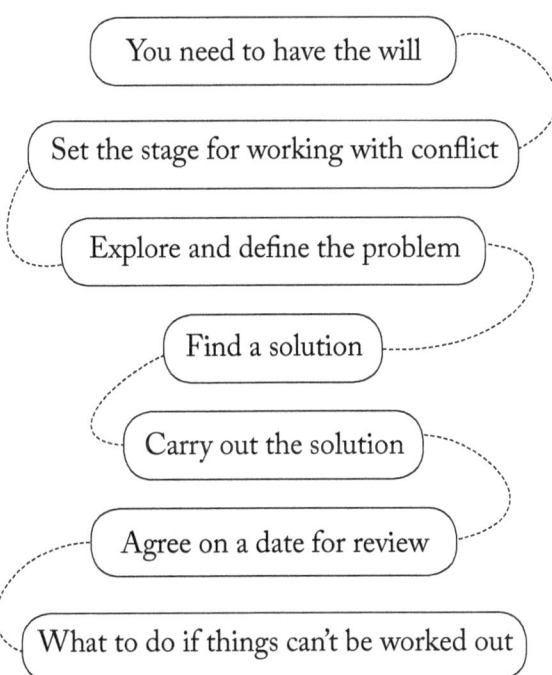

SUMMARY OF TOOLS AND GUIDELINES FOR RESOLVING CONFLICT

- You need to have the will
- Set the stage for working with conflict
- Explore and define the problem
- Find a solution
- Carry out the solution
- Agree on a date for review
- What to do if things can't be worked out

CONFLICT

SIGNS OF A PROBLEM WITH ANGER

Tick ☑ the signs that are familiar
- ☐ Feeling tense, on edge, and reactive much of the time
- ☐ Anger has become the first response to almost anything that 'goes wrong' or goes 'contrary to plan'
- ☐ Small annoyances trigger an angry response
- ☐ Reacting to some things in a way that is 'over the top' or excessive
- ☐ Blaming, accusing or criticising a partner or others is becoming frequent
- ☐ Anger about a particular issue builds up quickly and takes a long time to settle down
- ☐ Other emotions are not experienced much; they seem to merge into anger
- ☐ Feeling sometimes like smashing something, because of intense anger
- ☐ Shouting, screaming or yelling at a partner or children has become more frequent or intense, and is a concern
- ☐ Using anger to get people to cooperate, but there are bad feelings afterwards
- ☐ Being aggressive, threatening, and overly confrontational with other people
- ☐ Feeling like hurting oneself or someone else
- ☐ Expressing anger in violent behaviour

If some of these signs are familiar –

TAKE ACTION

Read thoroughly and apply the strategies in this section.

About Anger

Despite anger having had a lot of bad press, it is, nevertheless, a normal, natural, and useful human emotion. We experience anger in situations where we:

- feel powerless or 'forced into a corner'
- are mistreated or believe we have been mistreated
- are unable to feel in control in a situation we feel responsible for, or that needs to be brought under control
- have been made to feel embarrassed, or have been shamed or humiliated
- experience an event that taps into strong feelings unresolved from a situation that occurred in the past
- believe an injustice has been done to us or someone else we care about
- are fearful, but may not be fully aware of it.

The common denominator in all these situations is some sense of feeling *powerless*; and so the best use of the energy associated with anger is to direct it into what it is that is causing us to feel powerless.

> **Anger, if not given thoughtful direction, will find its own target.**

Anger is a powerful emotion that needs to be used thoughtfully and not unfairly targeted at ourselves or someone else.

Anger can be very helpful in:

- motivating us to find a solution to an injustice
- pushing us beyond our usual boundaries to examine how reasonable or fair our expectations of another person are
- causing us to face issues that may have been ignored previously, that need thought, decision, and action
- driving towards goals and constructively solving problems
- facing and dealing with things that are feared
- prompting us to communicate with others about how we feel and what we think about certain issues
- energising and motivating us to stand up for ourselves

- enabling us to accept or pursue major changes in our behaviour, priorities, or lifestyle.

Anger that lacks thoughtful direction, or that is simply 'bottled up' or covered over (such as with alcohol), has the potential to:

- grow in intensity
- become a more frequent and common response
- become more thoughtless and impulsive
- overshadow a person's whole behaviour and personality
- become explosive, violent, and destructive.

> **Frequent or chronic anger can lead to serious ill-health and relationship issues.**

Frequent or prolonged anger is associated with depression, anxiety, and insomnia, and a whole range of physical health conditions such as high blood pressure, suppressed immune system, ulcers, irritable bowel syndrome, heart disease, and stroke.

Anger that is not used appropriately (i.e. to solve problems and address issues) can be highly corrosive and damaging to relationships. It tends to leave little scope for conflict resolution, for compromise or concessions. It polarises people, reinforcing difference and disagreement, and escalating tension and ill-feeling.

Anger often displaces or devalues those aspects of a relationship that are so important to it being meaningful, like: respect, thoughtfulness, sensitivity, understanding, and empathy. Suppressed anger, when it finally cannot be contained any longer, often targets those who are least deserving of it, and is hugely out of proportion to the issue blamed as its cause.

Anger and the 'Fight or Flight' response

Feeling angry occurs in conjunction with a general experience of heightened mental and physical arousal, referred to as the 'fight or flight' response. This arousal is due to the body undergoing a series of biochemical changes in order to prepare us to deal with, or flee from, something that is perceived as a threat.

This was common in our more primitive past, when people frequently needed quick bursts of energy, as their bodies prepared to fight off or flee from ferocious predators or enemies. This remains an important response when we are faced with a real threat or danger. In other circumstances, it is less helpful, because it can also occur in response to threats that are imagined or thought to exist, and yet which do not.

Being too often in a state of 'fight or flight' can have serious health implications (already alluded to in reference to frequent or chronic anger).

The 'Fight or Flight' response

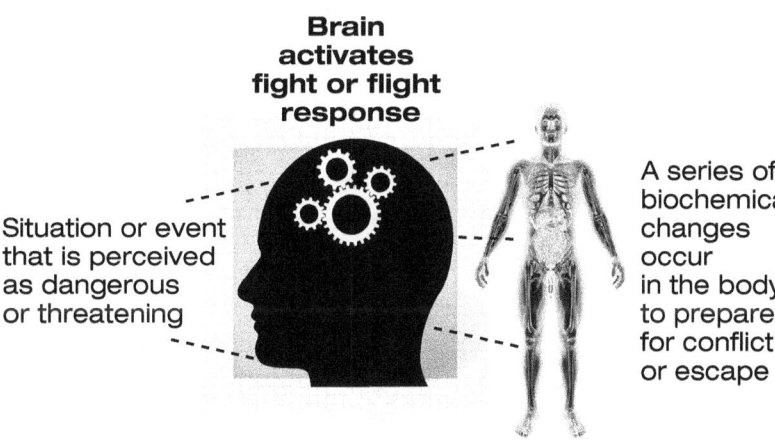

USING AND MANAGING ANGER EFFECTIVELY

To make good use of anger, it is important not to let it build up to the point where it is explosive, overwhelming, or out of control. It is vital to try to moderate anger if it is quickly building up, so that there is opportunity to consider what needs to be resolved and how (i.e. what generated the anger, and how the problem, threat or issue can be dealt with or resolved). There are some simple strategies that can be used for this:

STOP the escalation of anger –

- Decide not to retaliate, blame, accuse, or insult.
- Withdraw physically from the situation, if possible, to take some time to calm down and consider what has happened, and what to do.
- If you are unable to withdraw immediately and you are being verbally assaulted, 'needled' or provoked, activate an imaginary 'mind shield.' You can do this by electing a suitable 'switch' or 'button,' like touching or gently pressing the back of your neck with your finger, or pressing the tips of a finger and thumb together. When you do this, you can imagine a shield being activated that doesn't block your hearing, but does protect your mind, so that what is being said doesn't affect you.
- Remove yourself to a place where you can relax, and use a proven relaxation technique.

    Relaxation, particularly of a kind that releases muscle tension, can help turn off the 'fight or flight' response. The nerves in muscles that are relaxed change the type of signals they transmit to the brain. The brain then stops sending panic messages to the body's nervous system, and a general feeling of physical and mental calmness begins to prevail.

- For people who are often angry, there is little opportunity for high levels of muscle tension to diminish. The consequence of living with a high level of tension is that a state of tension becomes 'normal' and is taken for granted; so that being tense isn't noticed. Becoming aware of tension in our body, and taking steps to release it, is crucial to the management of anger – and to maintaining good mental and physical health.

> ### Recognising Tension
> *Ask yourself these questions:*
>
> - Where do I feel tension?
>   - In which parts of my body?
>   - In which muscles?
> - What does the tension feel like?
>   - Is there hardness?
>   - Is there fatigue?
>   - Is there an ache or pain?
> - What is it that has led to this tension?
> - Is this tension helpful or unhelpful?
> - Do I need to make time to relax?

CONSIDER what caused the anger and how the problem, threat or issue can be dealt with or resolved.

Why am I (or was I) angry?

The best use of anger is to direct it into the problem, threat or issue that is its source, thus avoiding directing it at ourselves or someone else. To trace anger back to its cause or source can usually be done by simply exploring:

- What happened – what was said or done that I perceived as a threat, a put-down, an embarrassment, or an injustice?
- What happened, has been happening, or is happening, that:
  - leaves me feeling powerless?
  - forces me into a corner?
  - puts me under unfair pressure?
- What has been done to me, has affected me, hurt, or threatened me, over which I have had little or no control?
- Is what has happened or is happening stopping me from doing what I think it is my role or responsibility to do?
- Do I feel angry because this is like something that has happened before or in the past, about which I still feel angry?

- Am I angry about a minor issue, which has unleashed stored up anger from other issues that I haven't properly faced or dealt with?
- Do I feel angry because another person has not done something I think he/she should have, or that I would have preferred? Are my expectations reasonable? Do I need to think about things from the other person's point of view?

What can I do about the problem?

How can the problem, threat or issue, that is the source of my anger, be resolved? Often anger can be resolved, and the 'fight or flight' arousal state turned off, simply by thinking constructively (rather than defensively), and working out how to deal with an issue. Taking the initiative can give us back a sense of being more in control, and is an effective antidote to feeling powerless.

On consideration of the source of our anger, it may turn out that we have 'jumped to conclusions,' not considered another person's point of view, or have had unfair or unreasonable expectations of them.

On the other hand, it may be that we have unreasonable expectations of ourselves, like always thinking: "I should," "I must," "I have to." If we are too rigid in what we expect of ourselves, sooner or later we will find ourselves unable to do what we think we must, and will feel threatened, powerless, and angry.

Other things to consider include:

- How could I try to explain or express to another person how I experienced something they have done?
- What kind of compromise could be made that respects both of our points of view?
- Do I need to consider a more formal process of conflict resolution?
- Am I angry about something that happened in the past that is really confusing or complicated, which I can't resolve without some professional support?
- Is the unfairness, injustice or cruelty that generates my anger, something I need to get support and expert advice in order to tackle?
- Do I need to use structured problem-solving with some of the issues?
- Am I calm enough and prepared enough to talk to the other person/people, and/or to tackle the issue with them?

ACT to try to resolve or address the issue/problem you have considered.

- Be determined but calm.
- Be clear about what you want – or don't want.
- Be flexible but not sidetracked.
- Stick to the issues (don't 'rope in' other issues).
- Be prepared to apologise if that is fair and appropriate.
- Seek the support, help or expertise of others, if that is needed and appropriate.

If you can't seem to get the issues resolved because of more anger, or because another person (or persons) can't agree or are not interested in your approach, go back immediately to:

STOP and then **CONSIDER**

REMEMBER

STOP

- Decide not to retaliate, blame, accuse, or insult
- Withdraw physically from the situation
- Activate a 'mind shield'
- Go somewhere to relax; become aware of and release tension

and/or

CONSIDER

- Why am I (or was I) angry?
  Where does it stem from?
    - Feeling powerless?
    - Unfair pressure?
    - Something happening/happened over which I have no control?
    - Unmet expectations?
    - Taps into an old issue or built up anger?
- What can I do about the problem?
    - Need to think constructively rather than defensively?
    - Do I have reasonable expectations?

- Have I jumped to conclusions?
- How could I try to explain how I feel?
- Compromise?
- Is a process of conflict resolution needed?
- Is this unresolvable without professional support?
- Do I need to problem solve the issue?
- Is this something that requires support and expert advice?
- Am I calm enough and prepared enough to act?

ACT

- Try now to resolve or address the issue/problem you have considered.
  - Be determined, calm, and clear about what you want – or don't want
  - Stick to the issue; don't be sidetracked, but be flexible
  - Be prepared to apologise if that is fair and appropriate
  - Get the support, help, or expertise of others if needed

Have you succeeded to a degree that the problem/issue no longer generates anger, or only generates energy and resolve useful to addressing the issue, or getting the problem solved?

YES ☐

NO ☐   go back to **STOP**
          and   **CONSIDER**

Further hints on managing anger

1. List the things that **trigger** your anger (from worst to least).
   Work on these things; seek to resolve them or rehearse how to respond to them better, *before* they occur again.
2. Practise the skills suggested (for using and managing anger effectively) with problems or issues that are easily manageable, in readiness for more difficult challenges later on.
3. Make getting plenty of sleep a priority. Sleeping poorly makes us much more susceptible to irritability and anger, and leaves us with little energy for tackling issues or problems constructively. If sleep is a problem, see the chapter on *Insomnia* (page 102).
4. Get regular daily exercise, dedicated to improving your mental and physical health (i.e. separate from work).
5. If you feel under a lot of stress, that may be contributing to your sense of powerlessness and your experience of anger. Consider some of the strategies for managing stress in the chapter on *Stress* (page 160).

What if nothing seems to work?

Sometimes it just doesn't seem possible to do anything about an issue or a problem that leaves us feeling angry. Yet, even though there may appear to be no way in which we can utilise anger to resolve an issue or problem, anger *can still be managed* and kept from being targeted at ourselves or others by:

- using a relaxation technique frequently
- exercising regularly
- resisting the urge to keep dwelling on the issue (with our thoughts and what we say to ourselves in our head)
- travelling to where we can speak to a skilled counsellor or psychotherapist (ask your doctor for a referral or recommendation)
- using a ritual, like writing about the source and experience of our anger, putting what we've written down in an envelope or container, and then placing it somewhere away from us – symbolically distancing ourselves from it, until we decide to revisit or abandon it.

If anger is caused by bullying, harassment or discrimination at work, or in dealing with a person or organisation, get some advice about your rights and how best to deal with the issues.

If you have tried to manage your anger and have failed, or if you are fearful of becoming (or have been) violent –

TAKE ACTION

Phone your nearest Community Health Service, or ask your doctor to recommend a skilled counsellor or psychotherapist.

For a man seeking such assistance, it is reasonable to ask for someone with experience and knowledge appropriate to working with men.

If no one suitable is available locally, make the trip to where there is someone who can provide skilled professional assistance.

Progressive Muscle Relaxation

A method of relaxation with proven effectiveness which relieves muscle tension, and can help switch off the 'fight or flight' anxiety response, is Progressive Muscle Relaxation. This involves tensing and then relaxing muscles in a step-by-step sequence. The two main principles of this technique include:

1. Tensing muscle groups (one at a time) to become aware of the feeling of tension.
2. Relaxing the muscles and feeling the tension in them subside – as if flowing out of the body.

Progressive Muscle Relaxation

- You will need about 15 minutes for this relaxation exercise.
- Find a quiet place where you won't be interrupted.
- Sit in a comfortable straight-backed chair, with your feet flat on the floor.
- Close your eyes and use the controlled breathing technique for about 5 minutes.
- Tense each of the following muscle groups for 5 seconds, then relax them completely for 15-20 seconds (pay particular attention to the different sensations of tension and relaxation):
    1. Curl both your fists and tighten your biceps and forearms (as if lifting weights). Relax.
    2. Wrinkle up your forehead; tighten the muscles in your face causing your face to wrinkle; purse your lips and press your tongue against the roof of your mouth; hunch your shoulders. Relax.
    3. Arch your back as you take a deep breath into your chest. Relax.
    4. Taking a deep breath, gently push out your stomach. Relax.
    5. Pull your feet and toes backwards tightening your shins. Relax.
    6. Curl your toes at the same time as tightening your calves, thighs and buttocks. Relax.
- Close your eyes and use the controlled breathing technique for about 5 minutes.
- Now resume normal activities in a calm and peaceful manner.

Tips and cautions on the use of Progressive Muscle Relaxation

- Be patient with yourself and this technique. You may experience only partial success at first. In time, it should be possible for you to relax your whole body quickly and successfully. Practise is the key.
- Be careful when you are tensing your neck and back.

    Excessive tightening could result in muscle or spinal damage. Over-tightening your toes or feet could result in muscle cramping.
- To achieve the best results with this technique, it is important to let go of the tension in a group of muscles you have tensed instantly. Releasing tension slowly may seem to relax muscles, when in fact it may just sustain tension. When you release muscle tension, do it instantly and let the muscles suddenly become limp.

Adapted from: Davis, M. et al. ***The Relaxation and Stress Reduction Workbook*** *Fourth edition (U.S.A., New Harbinger Publications, 1995) Chapter 4.*

WARNING SIGNS OF STRESS

Tick ☑ the signs that are familiar

- ☐ Problems getting to sleep and/or staying asleep
- ☐ Constant fatigue
- ☐ Poor concentration or forgetfulness
- ☐ Feeling fearful, anxious or overwhelmed
- ☐ Frequent urination
- ☐ Nervous diarrhoea
- ☐ Over-reaction to small things
- ☐ Frequent anger or frustration
- ☐ Light-headedness
- ☐ Lowered sexual desire and/or performance
- ☐ Muscle tension or pain
- ☐ Faintness, dizziness
- ☐ Poor appetite
- ☐ Being jumpy or easily startled
- ☐ Sweating, shaking, or nervousness
- ☐ Stomach cramps
- ☐ Shortness of breath without exercising
- ☐ Reduced work efficiency
- ☐ Over-use of alcohol or misuse of prescribed drugs
- ☐ Headaches or migraines
- ☐ Heartburn
- ☐ Moodiness
- ☐ Skin rashes

If you have some of these symptoms and they are affecting your life –

TAKE ACTION
Arrange to speak to a doctor

About Stress

We all know what it is to experience stress, and we usually have a pretty good idea of the kinds of things that seem to generate it (which are termed *stressors*). Trying to create a stress-free life would be both unrealistic and undesirable, since stress is associated with work, family, and personal relationships – in fact, with nearly all the changes and challenges that enable us to develop, adapt, and make our way successfully through life.

Some stress is actually quite beneficial to us, because it can generate energy, alertness, and motivation for a whole range of tasks. The problem arises when we experience too much stress at one time, or experience significant stress for a prolonged period of time. Severe or prolonged stress can have quite negative effects: it is associated with increased risk for many health problems (including some mental health problems):

- reflux, hyperacidity, heartburn, esophageal inflammation
- irritable bowel syndrome
- ulcers
- diarrhoea, constipation
- indigestion
- high blood pressure
- heart disease
- stroke
- bladder infection
- high cholesterol
- immune system related disorders
- asthma
- allergies and skin diseases
- colds and infections
- muscle spasm, muscle pains
- motility disturbance
- cancer
- neuro degenerative disorders
- fatigue

- anxiety
- depression
- insomnia
- alcohol and drug misuse and dependence
- concentration and memory problems.

Stress is far from being 'all in the mind,' since stressful events can trigger a whole series of biochemical changes in the body that are experienced physically as well as psychologically. And though the effects of stress differ from person to person, none of us is immune; no matter how 'easy going' we are, one day, it could affect us profoundly, especially if we're confronted by an unfamiliar and particularly difficult situation, which we don't have the coping resources to deal with.

Stress is an everyday fact of life. Its effects can be anything from minor and helpful, to severe and damaging. It can occur as a result of major life changes and challenges, or just the cumulative effect of many everyday worries.

The good news is: stress can be managed; it can be reduced and it can be kept at a level that is useful rather than harmful.

Stress management involves:

- Awareness and understanding
- Using stress reduction strategies
- Making healthy choices

SOURCES OF STRESS

There are a variety of sources from which we can experience stress, they include:

Our physical environment

We live in a dynamic, ever-changing and demanding physical environment. We are constantly responding and making adjustments to sounds, the weather (changes in temperature, humidity, and seasons; the possibility of flooding, drought, fire, and high winds), dangers, and challenges, in the course of moving about and travelling.

Our social environment

We have to cope with many social stressors, such as listening to and interacting with other people, work commitments, managing finances, dealing with disagreement and conflict, responding to many competing demands for our time, decision making and responding to problems, being interviewed or giving a speech, grieving losses of many kinds (perhaps including bereavement, separation/divorce, or loss of a job or livelihood), marriage, child rearing, and community commitments.

Life transitions and physical changes

We make transitions from childhood to adulthood to old age; from being single to being partnered; childless to having children; work to retirement. We experience many physical changes and challenges due to puberty, pregnancy, illness, menopause, old age, accident, sickness, inappropriate nutrition, lack of exercise, and sleep disturbance. There are also many body changes and symptoms that occur as a result of our reactions to threats and changes in our physical and social environments, such as: muscle tension, headaches and stomach upset, raised blood pressure, anxiety, and memory disturbance.

Our thoughts and self-talk

How our brain interprets and makes sense of life events, challenges, tasks, and experiences, if mostly or often negative, can be a significant source of stress for us. Because how we think and what we say to ourselves in our head (self-talk) are largely within our control, managing these thoughts is a very useful stress-reduction strategy (on which we will focus in this section). Though there are many sources of stress over which we have little control, we do have some choice about our thoughts and self-talk.

The 'Fight or Flight' response

Although there are many sources of stress over which we have little control (as already mentioned), how we interpret and make sense of life events, challenges, tasks, and experiences – and what we predict about the future from them – can serve either to simply engage us in a relatively calm response (even though perhaps feeling some emotion), or cause us to experience anxious arousal, more commonly referred to as being 'stressed.'

For example, if your friend is short with you and you don't hear from the person for a couple of days, it could be interpreted as meaning that something you have done (or not done) has caused the person to behave this way. This predicts for the future: ill feeling, avoidance, and all the pain of either trying to work things out or living with a broken friendship. This would be very anxiety-provoking or stressful; you would experience anxious arousal. But what if, alternatively, you simply viewed the person's behaviour as being due to tiredness or something bad happening at home? You would experience the person's behaviour quite differently. It would be unlikely to trigger much anxious arousal at all.

The experience of anxious arousal or stress is actually the effect of what has been termed the 'fight or flight' response.

When we are threatened by something or are in danger, our body responds with a series of biochemical changes aimed at preparing us to fight or escape. This was common in our more primitive past, when people frequently needed quick bursts of energy, as their bodies prepared to fight off or flee from ferocious predators or enemies. This remains an important response when we are faced with a real threat or danger. The problem is, our brain (in activating the 'fight or flight' response) does not distinguish between what is real and what is imagined.

Many novice public speakers would confess that giving a speech – even to a sympathetic audience – can generate as much terror and anxiety as any real physical danger or threat. What we imagine or perceive as threatening, and the way we anticipate problems or challenges in the future, whether real or not, may be 'real' enough for our brain to activate a response, and for us to feel stressed.

Severe stress is the result of the 'fight or flight' response occurring repeatedly for a prolonged period.

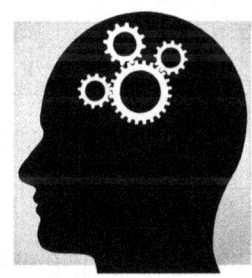

Brain activates fight or flight response

Situation or event that is perceived as dangerous or threatening

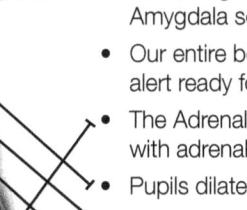

- Perceiving a threat, our primitive Amygdala sounds a general alarm.
- Our entire body is put in a state of high alert ready for fight or flight.
- The Adrenal system floods the body with adrenaline and stress hormones.
- Pupils dilate to better signal danger.
- Salivation is inhibited.
- Airways are relaxed – taking in more oxygen.
- Blood pressure and heart rate spike.
- Stomach and gastrointestinal tract constrict to divert blood to muscles.
- Bladder and colon prepare to void their contents in preparation for violent action and possible injury.
- Spleen contracts, pumping out white blood cells and platelets in preparation for potential physical injury.
- Hippocampus cements the response to the threat into long-term memory.

Changes that occur due to the 'Fight or Flight' response

- The mind becomes alert.
- Blood clotting ability increases, preparing for possible injury.
- Heart rate speeds up and blood pressure rises.
- Sweating increases to help cool the body.
- Blood is diverted to the muscles which tense ready for action.
- Digestion slows down.
- Saliva production decreases causing a dry mouth.
- Breathing rate speeds up – nostrils and air passages in lungs open wider to get in air more quickly.
- Liver releases sugar to provide quick energy.
- Sphincter muscles contract to close the openings of the bowel and bladder.
- Immune responses decrease (which is useful in the short-term to allow massive response to immediate threat, but can become harmful over a long period).
- Trembling or shaking
- Restlessness
- Cold and clammy hands
- Hot flushes or chills
- Feeling sick or nauseous
- Butterflies in the stomach

Excerpt from: **Management of Mental Disorders** Third edition (Australia, World Health Organization Collaborating Centre For Mental Health And Substance Abuse, 2000) Volumes 1 & 2.

Stress Reduction Strategies

There is a range of strategies that have proven to be helpful in the reduction and management of stress.

Those that are most effective in switching off the 'fight or flight' response are:

- **Relaxation**
- **Adopting constructive thought patterns** (revising how we interpret and make sense of life events)

Other important strategies include:

- **structured problem-solving**
- **restoring a pattern of normal sleep**
- **reducing alcohol and caffeine consumption**
- **making healthy choices.**

Relaxation

When we use a method of relaxation that can enable us to release tension in our muscles, the nerves in our muscles change the type of signals they transmit to the brain. The brain then stops sending panic messages to our nervous system, and a general feeling of physical and mental calmness begins to prevail.

For people who are often stressed, there is little opportunity for high levels of muscle tension to diminish. The consequence of living with a high level of tension is that a *state of tension* becomes 'normal' and is taken for granted; so that being tense isn't noticed.

Becoming aware of tension in our body, and taking steps to release it through effective relaxation, is a vital strategy for stress reduction.

> ## Recognising Tension
> ### *Ask yourself these questions:*
>
> - Where do I feel tension?
>   - In which parts of my body?
>   - In which muscles?
> - What does the tension feel like?
>   - Is there hardness?
>   - Is there fatigue?
>   - Is there an ache or pain?
> - What is it that has led to this tension?
> - Is this tension helpful or unhelpful?
> - Do I need to make time to relax?

Progressive Muscle Relaxation

A method of relaxation with proven effectiveness which relieves muscle tension, and can help switch off the 'fight or flight' anxiety response, is Progressive Muscle Relaxation. This involves tensing and then relaxing muscles in a step-by-step sequence. The two main principles of this technique include:

1. Tensing muscle groups (one at a time) to become aware of the feeling of tension.
2. Relaxing the muscles and feeling the tension in them subside – as if flowing out of the body.

Progressive Muscle Relaxation

- You will need about 15 minutes for this relaxation exercise.
- Find a quiet place where you won't be interrupted.
- Sit in a comfortable straight-backed chair, with your feet flat on the floor.
- Close your eyes and use the controlled breathing technique for about 5 minutes.
- Tense each of the following muscle groups for 5 seconds, then relax them completely for 15-20 seconds (pay particular attention to the different sensations of tension and relaxation):
  1. Curl both your fists and tighten your biceps and forearms (as if lifting weights). Relax.
  2. Wrinkle up your forehead; tighten the muscles in your face causing your face to wrinkle; purse your lips and press your tongue against the roof of your mouth; hunch your shoulders. Relax.
  3. Arch your back as you take a deep breath into your chest. Relax.
  4. Taking a deep breath, gently push out your stomach. Relax.
  5. Pull your feet and toes backwards tightening your shins. Relax.
  6. Curl your toes at the same time as tightening your calves, thighs and buttocks. Relax.
- Close your eyes and use the controlled breathing technique for about 5 minutes.
- Now resume normal activities in a calm and peaceful manner.

Tips and cautions on the use of progressive muscle relaxation

- Be patient with yourself and this technique. You may only experience partial success at first. In time, it should be possible for you to relax your whole body quickly and successfully. Practise is the key.
- Be careful when you are tensing your neck and back. Don't tighten your muscles beyond what feels comfortable for you.
- To achieve the best results with this technique it's important to let go of the tension in a group of muscles you have tensed instantly. Releasing tension slowly may seem to relax muscles, when in fact it may just sustain tension. When you release muscle tension, do it instantly and let the muscles suddenly become limp.

Adopting a constructive mental pattern

What we perceive as dangerous or threatening activates the 'fight or flight' response. When this perception changes – either because the danger or threat ceases, or because we alter the way we think about or interpret it ("This is not a threat or danger to me"), the 'fight or flight' response is de-activated – turned off.

How we interpret life events (the things that happen to us, challenge us, make demands of us, or that we perceive may have consequences for us), has a huge bearing on how much stress or anxiety we experience.

Part of this interpreting is what we think, how we think, and what we say to ourselves in our head (our self-talk).

The kind of mental pattern or way of interpreting events that we use is generally either **self-defeating** or, alternatively, **constructive**.

Self-defeating interpretations (thoughts and self-talk) can generate high and unhealthy levels of stress or anxiety – as well as causing paralysis in attempts at problem-solving and decision- making.

Constructive interpretations (thoughts and self-talk) help to maintain healthy and useful levels of stress or anxiety, which permit and promote coping.

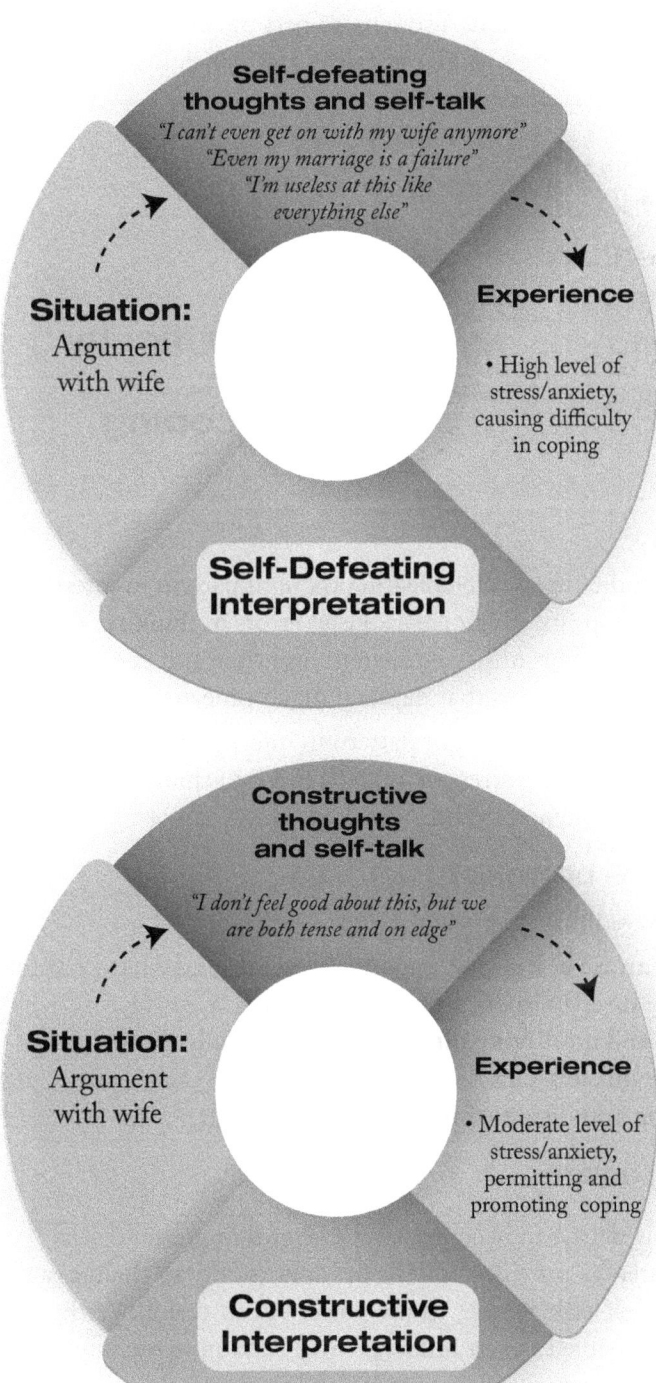

Self-defeating interpretations also tend to become more entrenched, and stress or anxiety levels more unhealthy and unhelpful, as a self-reinforcing vicious cycle develops.

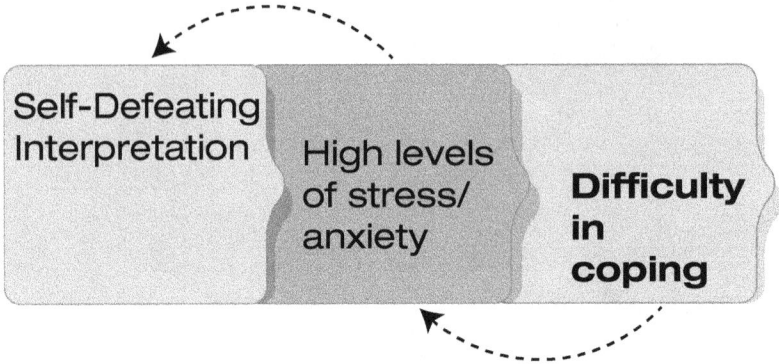

People who tend to use a self-defeating thought pattern in interpreting events also develop (mostly unconsciously) errors in thinking which, like jumping to conclusions, may seem to save time and energy, but can actually have consequences that demand much time and energy.

Adopting a constructive thought pattern in interpreting events is essential for managing stress or anxiety, and for achieving and maintaining good mental health.

How can this be done?

It can be achieved through:

- **becoming aware of how we respond to events** (and what we think and say to ourselves in our heads)
- **censoring and modifying our thoughts** (especially those that are automatic) **and self-talk**
- **challenging and dismantling errors in thinking.**

Becoming aware

We can simply decide to become aware of our thoughts and self-talk. This awareness provides us with the opportunity to change our thoughts and self-talk; it gives us the power of censorship. With practise, it is possible to exert influence over our automatic thoughts (challenging and dismantling errors in thinking will help this too).

To get this awareness underway, it is helpful to do some initial documenting of situations/events to be examined, the feelings experienced, and the thoughts that occur. This is also a good way of identifying errors in thinking.

Situation/event	Feelings experienced	Automatic thoughts (and self-talk)
You discover one of your vehicle tyres is flat, and you were organised to go somewhere.	Immediate 'welling up' of stress and anxiety, then strong feelings of anger.	"Everything just has to go wrong, like everything else around this place. I just don't need this."

Situation/event	Feelings experienced	Automatic thoughts (and self-talk)

Practising taking 'snapshots' of situations, and writing things down like this, is a useful tool for establishing awareness. After a while, this can be expanded into the skill of ***censoring and modifying*** thoughts and self-talk.

Censoring and modifying

The key to censoring and modifying (or managing) thoughts and self-talk is the speed with which we intervene and ask ourselves: Is this thought/idea (or what I've begun saying to myself) self-defeating or constructive? If it is self-defeating, how can I modify it immediately or replace it, so that I am using a constructive mental pattern?

This is a skill to be practised and a new habit to be formed. As with becoming *aware*, it can be really helpful (at least initially), to write things down; when we can 'see' our thoughts and what we are saying to ourselves, we have more power to change them.

Learning to manage thoughts:

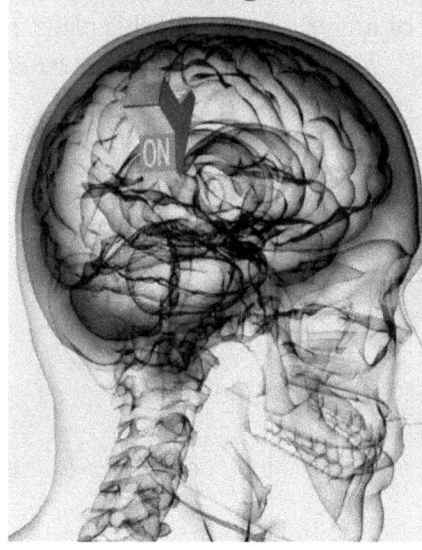

- ✓ Thinking rationally about challenges and problems
- ✓ Using structured problem solving
- ✓ Avoiding catastrophising
- ✓ 'Nipping in the bud' negative thinking
- ✓ Finding distractions when negative thinking occurs

Situation/event	My thoughts and self-talk	Are these self-defeating or constructive?	If self-defeating, what would be constructive?
A friend, who you had arranged to come over and help you with something important, has left a message to cancel.	"Why is it me that gets let down? This is typical of the way things go for me. One of these days something might just go right."	Self-defeating, because I have reacted negatively and feel more flat and depressed than before.	Considering: How do I know why he had to cancel? It could have been an emergency. I've cancelled things too. There are other things I can do; this can be put on hold. Everyone feels let down sometimes — that's life.
Situation/event	My thoughts and self-talk	Are these self-defeating or constructive?	If self-defeating, what would be constructive?
Situation/event	My thoughts and self-talk	Are these self-defeating or constructive?	If self-defeating, what would be constructive?

Challenging and dismantling errors in thinking

Errors in thinking consist of certain assumptions and ways of thinking that keep recurring, are habitual, and allow us to save time by not thinking *constructively* about events. They provide an easy response, but one that is neither time-saving nor helpful. Errors in thinking 'save a penny and spend a pound,' because their consequences heavily tax our energy reserves, and generate high and unhealthy levels of stress or anxiety.

Errors in thinking need to be challenged and revised if we are to establish a constructive and healthy mental thought pattern.

EXAMPLES OF COMMON ERRORS IN THINKING

Assumptions	Challenge
All things are equally important and urgent.	Many things are not crucial or urgent. But they generate anxiety because I interpret them that way.
	Some things are crucial and/or urgent and cannot be left. Many things are not, and they can be postponed.
Getting uptight about unforeseen or unwanted events is inevitable.	If I'm stressed or anxious, what does a thing matter, unless it is truly crucial or urgent?
	Getting up tight is not inevitable or necessary, it is a habit. Lots of other people take these things pretty much in their stride.
	No, getting uptight often is mostly because I often interpret events in a self-defeating way.

Assumptions	Challenge
Everything has to go wrong. Life is against me succeeding.	Based on what evidence? What about people who, against all apparent odds, still succeed? Do I need to examine how I go about things – how I make decisions, and for what reasons? If I expect things to go wrong, isn't it highly likely I will contribute to that happening? Has 'life' really singled me out to be a victim?
People always let me down.	What real evidence supports this assumption? Are other people let down also? How does my experience compare with theirs? Have I on occasions let others down? Do I know anyone who always experiences other people as completely reliable? Do I automatically believe the best or the worst when people appear to let me down? Are my expectations reasonable?

Assumptions	Challenge
If I could go back in time: If I had… If only I did…	The benefit of hindsight is a fine thing. Of course I could be more knowledgeable, skilled and wise if I could have been then who I am now, or if I could go back as who I am now. How is this kind of thinking helpful? I was who I was. I made decisions and did things as the person I was, and was capable of being **then**. No amount of lamenting will change that. The only valid questions are perhaps: What can I learn from the past? What can I do differently now and in the future?
Everything has to be done perfectly or properly	No one could live up to that, without lying about the many occasions when they, quite rightly, didn't bother to do some things either perfectly or properly. Taking pride in doing important things well is admirable. But trying to do everything perfectly or properly is not necessary, important, reasonable, or admirable. It is plain unhealthy! Perhaps what is more needful is to be able to prioritise?

Other thinking habits:

Mind-reading:	"She thinks I'm a failure;" "They think I'm not as good as..."
Catastrophising:	"Everything always turns out bad for me;" "Things are always against me;" "Now I will never be able to...;" "No matter how hard I try everything always goes wrong."
Labelling:	"I'm an idiot;" "I'm a failure;" "I'm a lousy..." (Instead of "I did... poorly;" or "I did not achieve...;" or "I needed to...")
Over-generalising:	Saying, "Always," "Never," "No-one," or "Everyone."
Fortune-telling:	"Everyone is sure to...;" "I'm sure to mess it up;" "It's going to be a disaster;" "I'm sure to feel dreadful when I..."
Rule-saying:	"Should," "Must," or "Have to" (setting sometimes unrealistic expectations).
Black and white thinking:	"Everything she does she gets right;" "I've completely ruined everything;" "He succeeds in everything... I never get it right!"

Examples you can think of:

....

....

....

....

STRUCTURED PROBLEM-SOLVING

For people who are stressed, it is common to feel threatened and overwhelmed by problems, and the thought of having to deal with them. So it can be really helpful to have a step-by-step methodical way of dealing with problems and making decisions. Through the method of structured problem-solving, it is possible to feel more in control of problems and to significantly reduce the feeling of being threatened or overwhelmed by them.

The **key elements** of this method include:

- Identifying and 'pinning down' the problems that have contributed to you feeling overwhelmed
- Thinking clearly and constructively about problems
- 'Taking stock' of how you've coped in the past: your personal strengths, and the support and resources available to you
- Providing a sound basis for important decision-making.

With this method you can work on a single problem or follow the process to tackle a number of problems.

Usually though – especially to begin with – it is best to deal with one problem that is specific and potentially solvable.

STRUCTURED PROBLEM-SOLVING INVOLVES 6 STEPS

Step 1
Write down the problem causing you worry or distress:

Step 2
Think about your options for dealing with this problem (try to think broadly – including good and not so good options); write them down:

1.	
2.	
3.	
4.	
5.	

Step 3
Write down the advantages and disadvantages of each option:

Step 4
Identify the best option(s) to deal with the problem:

1.	
2.	
3.	
4.	
5.	

Step 5 – List the steps needed to carry out each option (bear in mind the resources needed and pitfalls to overcome):

1. a.
b.
c.
2. a.
b.
c.
3. a.
b.
c.
4. a.
b.
c.
5. a.
b.
c.

Step 6

Review your progress in carrying out your option(s):

What have I achieved? ....

....

What still needs to be done? ....

....

RESTORING A PATTERN OF NORMAL SLEEP

Sleep disturbance is common with anxiety – particularly the problem of not being able to get off to sleep at night. To achieve a pattern of normal sleep, it is important to practise sleep-promoting behaviours during the day, in the evening, at bedtime, and during the night.

Better Sleep Guidelines

During the day

- Organise your day. Regular times for eating meals, taking medicines, performing chores and other activities, help keep our inner clocks running smoothly.
- Regular exercise during the day (or early evening) can improve sleeping patterns.
- Set aside time for problem-solving and decision-making during the day to avoid worry or anxiety at night.
- Avoid napping during the day – go to bed and get up at regular times.

During the evening

- Put the day to rest. If you still have things on your mind, write them down or put them in your diary, to be dealt with tomorrow.
- Light exercise early in the evening may help sleep. Avoid exercise late in the evening, as this may make getting to sleep more difficult.
- Get into a routine of 'winding down' during the course of the evening, allowing at least half an hour of quiet activity, such as reading or listening to music, prior to bedtime.
- Avoid drinking caffeinated drinks after about 4pm, and don't drink more than 2 cups of caffeinated drinks each day (especially coffee, tea, cocoa and cola).
- Avoid smoking for at least an hour (preferably an hour and a half) before going to bed.
- Don't use alcohol to make you sleep and keep your intake moderate (limit yourself to 2 standard drinks each day). Have 1 or 2 alcohol-free days each week.

- Make sure your bed and bedroom are comfortable – not too cold or too warm.
- Ensure that your bedroom is dark and that the morning light does not filter in. However, if you have a tendency to oversleep, it may be helpful to let the morning light into the room.
- Avoid a heavy meal close to bedtime. If you are hungry, a light snack might help you get to sleep.

At bedtime
- Try to do the same things before you go to bed each night. Develop a calming bedtime routine, such as having a warm bath or shower, listening to relaxation music, or using a relaxation technique. This way your body will learn to know that (with these activities) you are getting ready to go to sleep.
- Go to bed when you feel 'sleepy tired' and not before.
- Don't watch TV or have conversations or arguments in bed. Keep your bed and bedroom only for sleep (and sexual activity).
- Turn the light off when you get into bed.
- Relax and tell yourself that sleep will come when it is ready. Enjoy relaxing your mind and body, even if you don't at first fall asleep.

During the night
- If you wake up too early in the night, don't lie awake for more than 30 minutes. Instead of just being awake or worrying, get out of bed and do something that is distracting yet relaxing. Return to bed only when you feel sleepy again.
- Get up at the same time each morning. Don't sleep late in the morning trying to make up for 'lost sleep.'
- If you live in a place or area where there are sounds or noises that might wake you from sleep, have earplugs handy to block out the noise.
- Avoid sleeping pills – they do not provide a long-term solution to sleep problems.

REDUCING ALCOHOL AND CAFFEINE CONSUMPTION

The problem with alcohol and anxiety

It is common for people who are stressed to 'settle the nerves' or to cover over their fears using alcohol. There are several problems with this:

- Alcohol becomes a substitute for developing confidence.
- Dependence can quickly (but often unknowingly) occur, with alcohol being used for anxiety control in more and more situations.
- Usual coping strategies (even if only partially effective) become neglected and even less effective when alcohol is used as a substitute.
- Alcohol can negatively affect the quality of sleep, and interferes with the effects of medication prescribed for anxiety.

Strategies for moderating alcohol consumption

- Try to avoid drinking at home alone – especially when you are feeling down or anxious.
- Try limiting your drinking to the evening meal time.
- Drink low-alcohol beers and mixes.
- Drink slowly (limit yourself to 2 standard drinks each day).
- Think ahead (and creatively) about how to avoid drinking excessively in situations (like the pub or social gatherings) where there is pressure to do so.
- Plan to have 2 alcohol-free days each week. Try to choose days when it is easiest to do so, like when an activity is planned for the evening that may be a useful distraction.
- Decide how much alcohol you will permit yourself to drink; measure it out, and only allow yourself that amount.
- Always try to stay within the **Australian Alcohol Guidelines.**

For Men and Women

Over a lifetime: If you drink no more than 2 standard drinks a day, you reduce the lifetime risk of harming yourself from alcohol-related disease or injury.

On a single occasion: Having no more than 4 standard drinks on a single occasion reduces the risk of alcohol-related injury arising from that occasion.

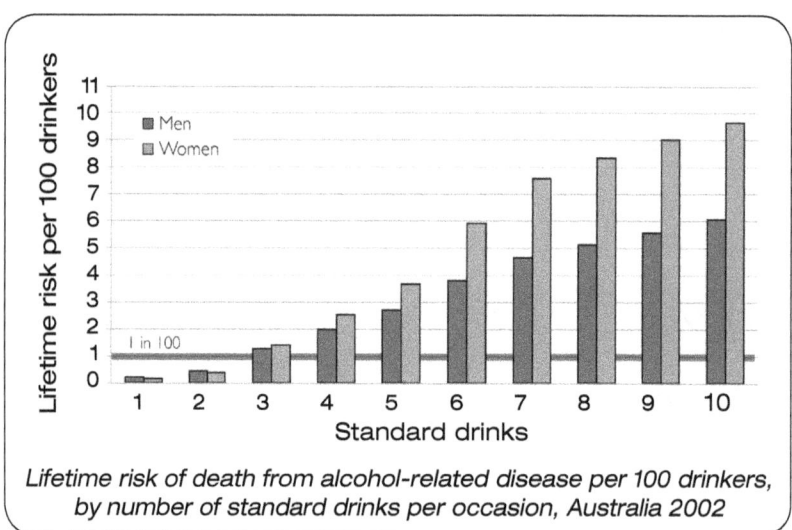

Lifetime risk of death from alcohol-related disease per 100 drinkers, by number of standard drinks per occasion, Australia 2002

people who regularly drink 2 standard drinks per day, the lifetime risk of death from an alcohol-related disease is about 0.4 in 100 people with that drinking pattern. Above that level, the risk increases with the number of drinks per day, and is above 1 in 100 at 3 drinks per day. The risk increases more sharply for women than for men.

Source: National Health and Medical Research Council Australian Guidelines to Reduce Health Risks from Drinking Alcohol, Canberra: Commonwealth of Australia, 2009.

The problem with caffeine and stress

Caffeine is a substance that is derived from plants or is produced synthetically, and is an additive in a number of food products and over-the-counter medications such as pain relievers, appetite suppressants, and cold medicines. Most commonly, it is known to be an ingredient in tea, coffee, chocolate, cocoa, colas, and so-called 'energy-boosting' beverages.

Tea and coffee are seen by most people merely as beverages, when in fact, they are actually vehicles for the psychoactive drug caffeine. Because caffeine is a central nervous system stimulant, in anxious people, it can worsen the symptoms of stress considerably.

People experiencing stress would do well to eliminate caffeine from their diet – or at least reduce their intake to a nominal amount. For tea and coffee drinkers, it is now possible to purchase these products in caffeine-reduced and decaffeinated forms. For people accustomed to a high caffeine intake, it is advisable to reduce consumption gradually to minimise potential withdrawal effects.

Making Healthy Choices

When people are stressed, it is often the simple things that are overlooked. And yet, it is the simple things that can often make the most difference to the level of stress we experience. Some of the following ideas may prove helpful.

Regular daily exercise

When we experience stress, our body produces the hormone adrenaline (part of the 'fight or flight' response). Left unused, adrenaline leaves us feeling 'wound up' or 'on edge,' our blood pressure will remain higher, and we will find it difficult to relax. Exercise can burn off this stress hormone, enabling us to relax.

The best kind of physical activity is separate from work, and dedicated purely to your physical and mental health. Walking, cycling, or using an exercise machine – even if for only 20 minutes several times a week, or when feeling stressed, can be quite beneficial.

Strengthen your relationships

Ironically, it is often when people are most stressed and need the support and stability of relationships, that they most neglect them.

Make it a priority to put quality time into strengthening and nurturing your relationships (with partner, friends, relatives, children). Make an extra effort to spend time with friends – particularly if they are in similar circumstances. You may be able to exchange helpful ideas, 'get things off your chest,' and feel less isolated and overwhelmed.

Find a positive way of 'letting off steam'

If you need to 'let off steam,' do it away from family or friends. Anger is very useful, if it is used for problem-solving, but it is destructive if we turn it on ourselves or others.

Make room for difference

Make room for difference in the way you and your partner see things, and especially in the way you deal with your feelings. Don't let stress exaggerate differences or make minor conflicts into issues that feel much bigger than they are.

Learn to say "no"

For people experiencing stress, it is often important to learn to say "no" (without feeling guilty) to new commitments or potentially stressful additional tasks or responsibilities. Say "yes" only to things you can achieve realistically.

Find a retreat where you can 'clear your head'

Find a place where you can go and be undisturbed, where you're able to feel calm, settled, and separated from the things that seem to be causing your stress. A place where, even if for only an hour, you can slow down and allow your body and mind to rest.

Reflect on what you value most

All of us would likely benefit from regularly stopping to consider what is really most important to us – what we value most. Too often, we can find that all our energy is taken up with things that are quite secondary to what is most important to us. For example, we can neglect our health and relationships because we allow other demands or priorities to 'jump the queue,' or overshadow everything else.

Relationship Violence

RELATIONSHIP VIOLENCE

Tick ☑ the signs that are familiar

Physical Violence
- ☐ Pushing, shoving
- ☐ Punching, biting, scratching, kicking, slapping
- ☐ Holding roughly, shaking, restraining
- ☐ Torturing, burning
- ☐ Throwing or smashing a partner's personal objects
- ☐ Hurting or killing a partner's pet
- ☐ Threateningly punching holes in a wall or door
- ☐ Throwing objects as weapons, such as dishes, glasses, ornaments, or other objects, that could do harm
- ☐ Threatening to use – or using – a weapon, such as a gun, knife, scissors, pan, shoe, or bottle, to hurt a partner
- ☐ Driving a vehicle, with a partner as a passenger, too fast or recklessly, to cause fear or to intimidate

Emotional and Verbal Violence
- ☐ Hurtful put-downs or name-calling
- ☐ Humiliating or shaming a partner
- ☐ Playing nasty, manipulative, or hurtful mind-games
- ☐ Making a partner frightened
- ☐ Constant nagging or needling
- ☐ Making a partner always feel bad about him or herself
- ☐ Disclosing embarrassing or private things about a partner in public, without your partner's consent
- ☐ Being very controlling or manipulative
- ☐ Using superior verbal skills to confuse, override, or intimidate a partner
- ☐ Involving/using children to manipulate or hurt a partner

Social Violence
- ☐ Not allowing a partner to choose his/her own friends
- ☐ Often speaking badly about a partner's family or friends
- ☐ Intentionally making a partner's family or friends feel unwelcome
- ☐ Humiliating, shaming, or belittling a partner in public
- ☐ Controlling a partner's every move; always checking-up on him/her; not allowing him/her to go out when he/she chooses

Financial Violence
- ☐ Not allowing a partner to have money
- ☐ Selling a partner's property, or property owned together, without his/her knowledge or permission
- ☐ Knowingly exploiting, manipulating, or taking advantage of a partner financially
- ☐ Making a partner beg, or behave in a manner against his/her will, for money
- ☐ Controlling or using a partner's finances (or finances held in common) against his/her will
- ☐ Shaming, belittling, or humiliating a partner because of his/her limited capacity to earn income

Religious Violence
- ☐ Trying to make a partner feel inferior or guilty because he/she doesn't, or doesn't want to, share the same beliefs
- ☐ Making a partner feel unsafe, frightened, inferior, humiliated, or personally compromised, by coercing him/her to participate in certain religious gatherings, rituals or ceremonies
- ☐ Using religious ideas, beliefs, threats, manipulation, or mind-games, to control a partner, exploit a partner sexually or financially, or cause him/her significant guilt, fear, or anxiety

Sexual Violence
- ☐ Forcing a partner to have sex against his/her will
- ☐ Being intentionally dishonest about the use of contraception
- ☐ Using drugs or alcohol in order to exploit a partner sexually

- ☐ Intentionally humiliating a partner sexually
- ☐ Using an object to violate a partner sexually
- ☐ Saying or insinuating hurtful or humiliating things about a partner's genitals or sexual performance – especially in the hearing of others

If some of these signs are familiar and you are concerned about your behaviour or the behaviour of your partner –

TAKE ACTION

| Speak to someone you trust, who can support you in thinking through what to do | Speak to your doctor | Phone a 24 hour Domestic Violence Help Line |

About Relationship Violence

Relationship violence is behaviour that violates, hurts, harms, humiliates, threatens, shames, manipulates, belittles, or frightens another person.

Both women and men sometimes resort to violence. Whoever uses it, is responsible for their own behaviour, for stopping their violence and, if need be, for obtaining professional assistance and support in order to stop it.

Whatever a partner's behaviour may be like – even if violent – it will not be resolved through a violent response. If a person's behaviour is hurtful, infuriating, or destructive to the relationship, then these issues and perhaps the future of the relationship need to be given honest consideration (which might require a lot of courage and some hard decisions). Ceasing violence should never be dependent on an expected change in a partner's behaviour. It needs to stop because it will achieve only harm, and will diminish very rapidly any chance of the relationship being salvaged.

Relationship violence, whether it's the behaviour of women or men, can be substituted with behaviours, strategies and skills that make room for tempers to calm, for issues to be tackled rationally, reasonably, and constructively – creating hope for the relationship rather than despair.

Relationship violence is often a sign that a relationship is heading into serious trouble and that problems exist that will very likely not be resolved without appropriate professional support and assistance. Once it is occurring, relationship violence usually worsens and becomes habitual.

Although there are some clear criteria for identifying relationship violence (such as physical or sexual assault, psychological trauma, or financial deprivation), what women or men experience as violating needs to be taken seriously and considered carefully. Furthermore, the simplistic distinction (still made in much literature on relationship violence) between victim and perpetrator is much less helpful than taking all the facts of a situation into consideration.

Making this distinction serves only to make matters worse, particularly in cases where both partners have used some form of violence. By distorting the reality of what has been happening, it is likely that the kind of solutions applied to the problem will be unfair (inequitable), inappropriate, and destructive, rather than helpful to the future of the relationship.

In circumstances of significant or persistent violence, partners may need to be separated, or one partner helped to stay in alternative safe accommodation, while sense is made of what has been happening, and genuinely helpful options for support and assistance are considered.

Feeling unsafe or that things are unsafe for children should never be ignored. This is especially the case where people are geographically isolated. If the situation becomes worse, there may not be enough time to prevent something bad happening, because of the distance someone must travel to get or give help.

How to help someone else

You may know of a relationship in which violence is occurring, but don't know what to do. There are several things to keep in mind here:

- Think about how you could help (and what you might need to do) that won't create a risk for your safety.
- Don't offer to help unless you are prepared for a potentially frustrating, confusing and draining situation.
- Think about who could give *you* extra support while you're helping others.

Ways of helping

- Express clearly your concern about what is happening.
- Avoid imposing your own view or opinions about what they should do.
- Help them understand and take the violence seriously; including what it might mean for their relationship if it continues (remember relationship violence often worsens and becomes habitual).
- Be a good listener and avoid being impatient (even if little progress seems to be made).
- Be encouraging and supportive, but avoid being critical of the other partner.
- Help them to understand that it is not a betrayal, cowardly, or weak to take measures to stop the violence. It puts a value on their relationship and on themselves to take action, even if to do so is at first embarrassing, upsetting, or hard.
- Be sure to consider carefully their safety and your own. If need be, draw up a safety plan.
- Help them to obtain the very best professional support and assistance available. Perhaps offer to go with them to see a counsellor, or speak to a doctor or the police.
- Offer to help obtain any information that may be needed by them, to be able to make sound, well-informed decisions about things.
- Don't take over; don't pressure them into decisions; don't do things without their consent.

- If the situation is becoming unsafe, is immediately unsafe, or is feeling unsafe, encourage them to contact the police (or offer to do so yourself). If using some other means of achieving safety (such as arranging for a friend to come and take them to safety, or driving themselves to a safe place), ensure that risks are properly considered and assessed before doing so.

ALCOHOL

Information in this chapter has been based on valuable information from the Australian Drug Foundation (www. adf.org.au).

Signs of a problem with Alcohol

Tick ☑ the signs that are familiar

- ☐ Using alcohol to cope with stress, anxiety, anger, or sleeplessness
- ☐ Regularly drinking more than 4 drinks on one occasion
- ☐ Have tried to cut down or stop drinking without success
- ☐ Sometimes fail to do what is normally expected of you because of drinking
- ☐ Feeling uneasy, guilty, or remorseful about the amount of alcohol being consumed
- ☐ Feeling especially hopeless, angry or sad, following a bout of drinking
- ☐ Behaviour after a bout of drinking that is later regretted
- ☐ Have been injured (or have injured someone else) as a result of drinking
- ☐ Drinking is followed by conflict or arguments with a partner
- ☐ Being unable to stop drinking once having started
- ☐ A friend, relative, or a doctor has expressed concerns
- ☐ Unable to remember what happened the night before because of drinking
- ☐ Sometimes start drinking early in the day as a way of 'steadying the nerves,' or getting rid of a hangover

If some of these signs are familiar –

TAKE ACTION

READ:
About Alcohol and, **Doing Something About It,** to consider your options and to decide what to do

Speak to your doctor

VISIT or PHONE:
refer to contact information on page 197

MY CONTRACT

Cutting Down or Cutting Out

I can make decisions that affect my lifestyle and well-being

I will stop drinking entirely from ..../.............../20..............

OR

I will stop drinking for a period of .... weeks starting from ..../.............../20..............

AND/OR

From ..../.............../20.............. I will cut down drinking and drink no more than .... a day/week/etc

About Alcohol

Alcohol is actually a central nervous system depressant and not a stimulant as popularly believed. It slows the activity of the central nervous system, affecting concentration and coordination, and slowing the response time to unexpected situations.

In small doses, alcohol produces relaxation, a lowering of inhibitions, feelings of confidence, and more 'outgoingness'. In larger doses, alcohol can cause unconsciousness and death.

The effects alcohol can have on health and well-being

Drinking too much alcohol on a regular basis can affect a person's health and well-being in a range of ways. The effects of alcohol can also vary depending on a range of factors such as:
- age
- body size
- how recently you have eaten
- medications you are taking
- whether you are a man or a woman
- level of fitness
- health of your liver.

Some of the immediate or short-term ways alcohol affects health and well-being include:
- Reduced coordination, slower reflexes and poor muscle control which may increase your risk of falling or having an accident
- Reduced inhibition, more intense moods and impaired judgement which may mean that people might react uncharacteristically or get involved in situations in which they wouldn't normally become involved (i.e. fights)
- Difficulty concentrating and memory disturbance
- Disturbed sleep
- Sexual dysfunction
- Worsened depression, anxiety, and chronic stress
- Nausea and vomiting
- Coma and death.

Long-term effects can include:
- Liver disease, including swelling and pain, cirrhosis and cancer
- Brain damage and memory loss
- Cancer, including breast, mouth, throat, and oesophagus cancers
- Worsened depression, anxiety, and chronic stress
- Heart and circulatory problems, including high blood pressure
- Stomach, bowel and pancreas problems, including inflammation, bleeding and ulcers
- Alcohol dependence.

The benefits of alcohol on health

There is some evidence to suggest that, for middle-aged and older people, there are health benefits to be had from drinking regularly very small amounts of alcohol (within Guideline 1). However, the benefits that regular drinking of a small amount of alcohol might have on cardiovascular disorders can also be achieved through a healthy diet, regular exercise, and not smoking.

Reducing alcohol related risks and harms

The *Australian Guidelines to Reduce Health Risks from Drinking Alcohol* provide 4 guidelines for people to reduce the risk of harm associated with drinking alcohol.

GUIDELINE 1:

Reducing the risk of alcohol-related harm over a lifetime

The lifetime risk of harm from drinking alcohol increases with the amount of alcohol consumed.

For healthy men and women, drinking no more than 2 standard drinks on any day reduces the lifetime risk of harm from an alcohol-related disease or injury.

If this guideline is followed, the lifetime risk of death from alcohol-related disease or injury for both men and women remains below 1 in 100. Every drink above this level increases this lifetime risk of both disease and injury and drinking less on each occasion reduces the risk.

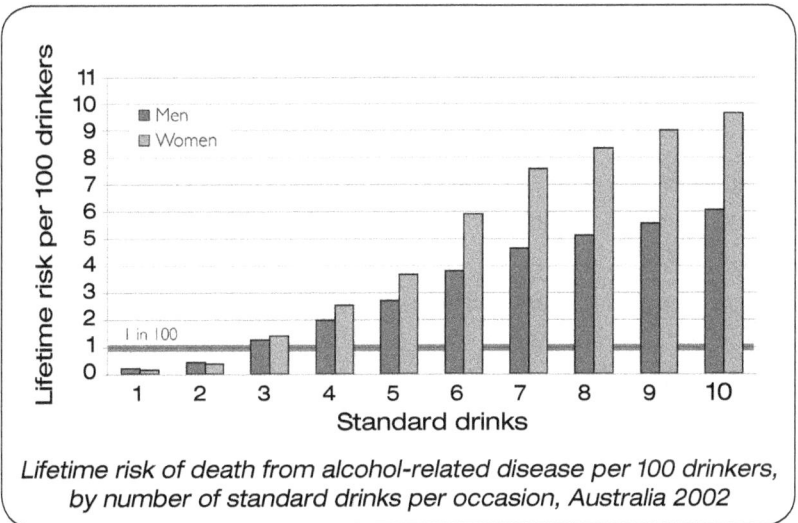

Lifetime risk of death from alcohol-related disease per 100 drinkers, by number of standard drinks per occasion, Australia 2002

For people who regularly drink 2 standard drinks per day, the lifetime risk of death from an alcohol-related disease is about 0.4 in 100 people with that drinking pattern. Above that level, the risk increases with the number of drinks per day, and is above 1 in 100 at 3 drinks per day. The risk increases more sharply for women than for men.

Source: National Health and Medical Research Council Australian Guidelines to Reduce Health Risks from Drinking Alcohol, Canberra: Commonwealth of Australia, 2009.

GUIDELINE 2:

Reducing the risk of injury on a single occasion of drinking

On a single occasion of drinking, the risk of alcohol-related injury increases with the amount consumed.

For healthy men and women, drinking no more than 4 standard drinks on a single occasion reduces the risk of alcohol-related injury arising from that occasion.

Drinking 4 standard drinks on a single occasion more than doubles the relative risk of injury in the 6 hours afterwards. This risk increases rapidly when more than 4 drinks are consumed.

Each drinking occasion also contributes to the lifetime risk of alcohol-related harm (see Guideline 1, opposite).

GUIDELINE 3:

Children and young people under 18 years of age

For children and young people under 18 years of age, not drinking alcohol is the safest option.

Parents and carers are advised that children under 15 years of age are at the greatest risk of harm from drinking and that for this age group, not drinking is especially important.

For young people aged 15–17 years, the safest option is to delay the initiation of drinking for as long as possible.

GUIDELINE 4:

Pregnancy and breastfeeding

Maternal alcohol consumption can harm the developing fetus or breastfeeding baby.

For women who are pregnant or planning a pregnancy, **not drinking is the safest option.**

For women who are breastfeeding, not drinking is the safest option.

These guidelines provide a general guide and there are a number of additional issues to take into account when thinking about your drinking. For example:

Not drinking is the safest option when involved in, or supervising, any activity involving risk or a degree of skill, such as:
- driving
- flying
- skiing
- water sports
- using heavy machinery, farm machinery, or power tools
- supervising children.

Some people should get advice about drinking because of possible interactions and harmful effects. This includes people who:
- are taking medications (including over-the-counter or prescription medications)
- have alcohol-related, or other physical, conditions that can be made worse or affected by alcohol
- people with mental health conditions.

Some groups should be aware that they can be at increased risk of harm if they drink. This includes:
- young adults aged 18–25 years
- older people aged over 60 years
- people with a family history of alcohol dependence
- people who use drugs illicitly.

What is a standard drink?

The amount of alcohol in alcoholic drinks varies. A standard drink is defined as one that contains 10 grams of pure alcohol.

How do you line up against these guidelines?

- If you are drinking within the recommended guidelines, you are reducing the risk of experiencing alcohol-related harm.
- If you are drinking more than is recommended by the guidelines, read on to consider how to reduce your drinking and the risk of experiencing alcohol-related harms.

Some common questions about alcohol

1. *Does drinking affect sexual performance?*

Yes. Heavy drinking can cause sexual dysfunction. Most men are aware of the link between alcohol and erectile problems.

2. *Is beer fattening?*

Yes. Alcohol is high in calories and contains few nutrients or vitamins. Drinking beer, or any other alcoholic drink, adds calories to a person's diet which can result in a person gaining weight and lead to obesity.

3. *Can I save up my drinks for one good session?*

No. Drinking more than 4 standard drinks on a single occasion more than doubles the relative risk of experiencing an injury in the following 6 hours. This risk increases rapidly when more than 4 drinks are consumed. Each drinking occasion also contributes to the lifetime risk of alcohol-related harm (see Guideline 1 & 2, on page 181 & 182).

4. *Can I drink when I'm on medication?*

Mixing alcohol with medications (either over-the-counter or prescription) can have unexpected and even dangerous effects. There is also the risk that alcohol may affect how well the medication works.

It is important to read the packaging and consumer medicines information sheet and to talk to your doctor or pharmacist about the potential effects alcohol and other drugs may have on your medication.

5. *Can alcohol help sleep?*

No. Though alcohol may help you to feel tired and to go to sleep, it usually causes disrupted and poor quality sleep.

6. *How does alcohol affect mental health conditions?*

The relationship between alcohol and mental health conditions is complex. As a general rule, they do not mix well. Alcohol can interfere with the effectiveness of many medications and can be dangerous when taken in combination with others.

Alcohol may even increase the risk of conditions such as depression and anxiety in some people. It may also worsen, rather than help, symptoms and can increase the risk of violence and suicidal behaviour.

7. *Should pregnant women drink alcohol?*

The World Health Organization and the *Australian Guidelines to Reduce Health Risks from Drinking Alcohol* note that there is no known safe level of drinking alcohol during pregnancy and breastfeeding.

The safest option for women who are pregnant or planning a pregnancy is not to drink alcohol.

8. *Should women who are breastfeeding avoid alcohol?* As mentioned above, there is no known safe level of drinking alcohol while breastfeeding. Therefore, the safest option for women who are breastfeeding is not to drink alcohol.

9. *Am I at risk of developing an alcohol-related problem if my family has a history of alcohol problems?*

Yes. This does not mean you will develop an alcohol-related problem, but having a family history of alcohol-related problems is one of the factors that increase the risk.

The degree of risk is related to:

- the closeness of the relative who has the alcohol-related problem
- the number of relatives involved.

Knowing your family's health history can help you understand and make informed choices about your drinking and the potential risks.

10. *Can you drink the same amount as you get older?*

The older you get, the less well your body can 'handle' alcohol. Changes in the body's makeup and metabolism and increased use of medications as we age, affects the way older people process alcohol. Alcohol can increase the risk of falls, accidents while driving, and suicide in older people. Some medications, when used in combination with alcohol, can also further increase these risks as well as reduce the effectiveness or increase the side-effects of the medications.

DOING SOMETHING ABOUT IT

Now that you know your risk level (and the issues for your health at that level), you can decide to:

- **continue as you are** OR
- **reduce your drinking by either drinking less or stopping altogether**.

Before you decide, consider the positives and negatives using the Balance Sheet:

Continue Present Drinking Pattern	
Positives	Negatives
A couple of drinks helps me feel comfortable when out and meeting new people	Takes a while to recover the next day from hangover
Change Present Drinking Pattern	
Positives	Negatives
Not arguing about alcohol with partner	Not being able to have a couple of drinks after work with mates

On balance, do you think you need to do something about your drinking?

NO ☐   YES ☐

Read On....

Cutting down or cutting out?

So, at this stage you know your risk category and have decided to do something about your drinking levels. Your next decision is whether you'll drink less – or cut out alcohol altogether.

To help you make up your mind, think about the following questions:

- ☐ Do you have any health problems that might be made worse by alcohol? Your doctor can advise you.
- ☐ Have you solved your drinking problems before by stopping completely? Then this might be your best way now.
- ☐ Are you convinced you will never be able to drink sensibly and safely? Cutting out could be your answer.
- ☐ Once you start drinking, do you have difficulty stopping? Cutting out could be your answer.

It is a good idea to have a chat to your doctor about your drinking. Doctors can provide advice, information, assistance and support. They can also help you cope with any withdrawal symptoms you might experience and if required, discuss different treatment options and provide referrals to other services.

Consider the positives and negatives of cutting down or cutting out alcohol using the Balance Sheet:

Cutting Down	
Positives	Negatives
Can still have the occasional drink with friends?	Not sure I can stop once I start
Cutting Out	
Positives	Negatives
No risk of losing track of how much I have drunk	People will laugh at me and think I'm strange for not drinking anything

What is your decision?

- ☐ To cut down your drinking?
- ☐ To cut out drinking for a while?
- ☐ To cut out drinking entirely?

What you decide here might not be the decision you follow for the rest of your life. You can review your drinking goal whenever you want to.

Whatever you decide, confide in the person you are closest to, tell him/her your goal, and get his/her support.

If you need professional assistance to help you choose the best goal, speak to your doctor, or contact one of the following alcohol and drug information services:

NATIONAL: For information, call the Druginfo Clearinghouse on 1300 85 85 84

ACT	(02) 6207 9977
QLD	1800 177 833
NSW	1800 422 599
	(02) 9361 8000 (metro area)
NT	1800 131 350
SA	1300 131 340 (08) 8363 8618
VIC	1800 888 236
TAS	1800 811 994
WA	1800 198 024
	(08) 9442 5000 (metro area)

Cutting out alcohol for a while

People decide to cut out alcohol for different reasons, and they often have different long-term goals. Some people want to stop drinking forever; others just need a break from it. No matter what your reasons or what your long-term goals are, the main job ahead of you now is to focus on your goals and work towards achieving them.

Will I experience withdrawal if I stop drinking?

If you are a heavy drinker and you are dependent on alcohol, you may experience withdrawal if you stop drinking suddenly.

Mild withdrawal symptoms may include:

- nausea
- sweating
- poor sleep
- loss of appetite
- the 'shakes'
- restlessness, agitation and irritability.

Severe withdrawal symptoms may include:

- vomiting
- disorientation
- having fits
- fever
- hallucinations
- coma (with a small risk of death if not treated with medication).

People who experience severe withdrawal symptoms should consult their doctor immediately.

If you are a heavy drinker or you are dependent on alcohol, speak to a doctor or health professional at an Alcohol and Drug Service, before you start cutting out alcohol. Supervised withdrawal may be necessary.

Make a contract with yourself

If you have decided to cut down or cut out drinking, why not make a contract with yourself? You can also show it to a close friend, partner, or family member who can help remind you of the contract and why you are changing your drinking patterns if things get tough.

Planning ahead to minimise failure

If you can identify the occasions where you drank more than you meant to, or badly wanted a drink, it will help you to plan ahead to minimise or avoid the chances of you drinking or drinking more than you planned.

Think about the situations in which you are at highest risk of drinking?

For example:

- Are your high-risk situations in particular places (like home)?

Or around certain people; certain family members? Or at particular times, like after dinner?

- Are high-risk situations also tied to certain emotions – when you feel depressed, angry, irritable, on edge, worried, guilty?

- Think of the last few times when your drinking got you into trouble… and when it didn't. What is the difference between these occasions?

Some examples of risky situations may include:

- when I have had a row with someone in the family
- when someone has been having a go at me and I feel like a failure
- when I am out at the pub and I feel uncomfortable if I'm sober.

Everyone is unique and has different risky situations. Perhaps you could think of your own high-risk situations and write them down.

My main high-risk situations are:

VERY IMPORTANT...

1 ....
2 ....
3 ....
4 ....

Now that you have worked out when and why you might drink a lot, how could you cope in these situations without a drink in your hand? Instead of waiting until you are under pressure, it is best to plan ahead and prepare some useful strategies for coping.

In working out some strategies for coping, bear in mind that:

- they need to be well thought-out and realistic
- you may need to be quite creative and think of things you haven't tried before
- you may need courage to carry them out but, if they are too difficult or need too much courage, you probably won't use them.

List your main high-risk situations again, but this time, with some strategies for coping with them.

My main high-risk situations are:	My strategies for coping are:
When I have had a row with someone in the family	To take the dog for a walk to the park
1.	1.
2.	2.
3.	3.
4.	4.
5.	5.
6.	6.
7.	7.
8.	8.
9.	9.
10.	10.

Setting your own drinking guidelines

If your drinking goal is to cut out alcohol entirely, your guidelines are clear-cut:

...NO ALCOHOL IN ANY SITUATION.

If your goal is cutting down, you will need to set some guidelines like these:

- ☐ how many days a week you'll be drinking
- ☐ how much you'll have on your drinking days
- ☐ how many alcohol-free days you'll have each week
- ☐ high-risk situations where you'll avoid drinking altogether
- ☐ having at least two strategies to deal with high-risk situations
- ☐ know who your mates and/or supporters are; the ones you can rely on to help you through.

NOTES

My Drinking Guidelines Are

1. Circle the day(s) I will have as **alcohol-free** (ideally 2 days a week)

    Monday   Tuesday   Wednesday
    Thursday   Friday   Saturday   Sunday

2. My limit of standard drinks on any one drinking day is ....

3. On average I will drink no more than .... standard drinks per day which equals a limit of .... standard drinks per week.

4. My personal goal is ....

5. High-risk situations I will avoid altogether are ....
   ....
   ....

6. Other high-risk situations and strategies for coping are:

High-risk Situations	Strategies for Coping
1.	a.
	b.
2.	a.
	b.
3.	a.
	b.
4.	a.
	b.

> I will not be hard on myself if I don't always achieve these goals – but I will keep trying

ALCOHOL

Practical Tips for Cutting Down or Cutting Out

- Practise saying: "**NO THANKS.**" It may be difficult at first, but you will be surprised how quickly it can become comfortable to say "NO". Others might appreciate it.

If you have always said "YES" in the past, it can be hard to say that first "NO". But once you have taken the plunge, you will be pleasantly surprised how easy it becomes to refuse a drink, and you will feel good about yourself too.

A simple **"No thanks, I don't feel like drinking"** is effective. Or you can say……..

"No thanks, I'm cutting down."

"No thanks, I'm having a rest from drinking for a while." "No thanks, I'm taking some medication that means I can't drink."

"No thanks, I'm OK for now, but let me buy you one." "No thanks, I've had my limit" or **"I've had enough."**

If people keep pushing drinks onto you, ask yourself why they are doing it. Maybe they feel more comfortable about their own drinking if you drink like them. If this is a high-risk situation for you, perhaps you need to avoid it.

- **Try low-alcohol alternatives.** Try the range of low and medium-strength beers, or dilute your wine and/or spirits to make your drinks last longer.
- **Eat before or while you are drinking.** With food in your stomach, you are likely to drink more slowly and the alcohol is absorbed into your bloodstream at a slower rate.
- **Take less alcohol with you.** When you go out, you tend to drink what you take with you. Take less and drink less.
- **Count your drinks.** Remember to maintain your drink diary. Check the label on the bottle or can of alcohol – it will tell you how many standard drinks it contains. If you are drinking stubbies, bottles or cans, put the caps and ring pulls in your pocket so you can keep a count of how many you have drunk.
- **Slow down your drinking.** You'll enjoy your drink just as much, maybe more, if you drink it slowly. Sip, don't gulp. Try to sit on a schooner for about 30 minutes. This will help you control your rate of drinking. Concentrate on drinking every drink slowly.

- **Make every second drink a non-alcoholic drink.** Drink soft drink, water, or fruit juice as 'spacers.' You will find that by having a drink in your hand, even a soft drink, you won't feel left out.
- **Drink water with a meal.** Have water available on the table while you are having a meal.
- **Use a smaller glass or add more non-alcoholic mixer.**
  If you normally have a large beer (i.e. a pint), have a small glass and drink it slowly. If you make your own mixed drinks, use less alcohol.
- **Avoid top-ups.** With top-ups, you can't be sure how much you are drinking.
- **When you are thirsty, have a soft drink or water first.**
  By quenching your thirst, you will be able to drink your alcohol more slowly.
- **Stop drinking when you have reached your limit.** Start drinking soft drinks, fruit juice, etc. You'll find that you can do without that extra drink after all.
- **Avoid drinking in rounds and 'schools.'** Set your own drinking pace. The following strategies can help you avoid drinking a 'round':
  - Simply opt out. Say you just don't want to join the round.
  - Join the round, but occasionally order a non-alcoholic drink for yourself as a spacer.
  - Buy a round (to show your generosity), but then opt out and buy your own. You may pay a bit more, but you don't harm your health.
  - Pass up a drink during the round; your friends won't mind, you're saving them money.

  If the suggestions for drinking in rounds or schools are too difficult, avoid the situations where the pressure is on you to drink in groups.
- **Avoid drinking situations.** Go to places where they don't serve alcohol. By choosing to cut down on your drinking, you may need to find new ways to entertain yourself. If you drink because you are bored or stressed, try taking a walk or calling a friend instead.

Coping with slip-ups

If you do slip-up, it doesn't have to be the end of your efforts.

Lapses and slip-ups are normal!

The worst thing to do is to blame yourself for being weak or to start thinking you've failed. Don't throw in the towel. You might just have to revise your strategies or your drinking guidelines and continue.

By making these slips, we learn how to avoid future pitfalls; when you lose, don't lose the lesson! Think about what caused you to slip-up and find ways of dealing with it in the future. Discuss it with your supporter, your mates, or a health professional. Look at the drinking tips and remind yourself of your reasons for cutting down. Review your determination to succeed.

If you do resume your regular old drinking patterns, don't despair. Don't give up your intention to cut down on your drinking. Most people who want to change will make several serious attempts before they reach their goals.

Be kind to yourself if you do slip and haven't achieved all your goals. Remind yourself of current research that says that change doesn't happen overnight. Be patient.

Look at your goals and plans and think about why you have gone back to your old drinking patterns. Revise your goals and plans and try again.

Remember, small steps in the right direction take you closer toward your goal.

Substances and Mental Health

SUBSTANCES AND MENTAL HEALTH

Dangers of illicit substance use

People who use illicit substances are more than twice as likely to have a serious mental health difficulty as those who do not use illicit substances.

Though there are far fewer users of illicit substances in comparison to users of nicotine and alcohol, the mental health consequences of illicit substance use are a very serious problem.

Approximately 1,000 deaths and 119,000 hospitalisations in 2013 – 2014 have been associated with illicit substance use. But this is not a clear indication of the effects these substances have on mental health. It simply hasn't been possible to establish a clear picture of the magnitude of these effects, because many people with a mental health difficulty associated with illicit substance use remain undiagnosed and untreated. It is also often impossible to tell which problem came first, the drug problem or the mental health difficulty. Many people do develop drug problems in an attempt to deal with their depression or anxiety.

What we do know is that the use of illicit substances can play a significant role in causing and maintaining, anxiety, depression, paranoia, confusion, panic, psychosis, and other problems. The use of these substances can also:

- conceal or obscure the symptoms or presence of a mental health difficulty from those who could help you
- worsen the symptoms of mental health difficulty
- inhibit recovery from mental health difficulty
- interfere with the effectiveness of prescribed medication
- interact dangerously with some prescribed medications.

Am I dependent?

Dependent has replaced 'addicted' in medical terminology. It is important to consider whether you are dependent as this can be more difficult to address and have a great impact on your mental state.

Generally, you are dependent on a substance if you:
- continue to use the substance despite it causing problems for you or others.
- have tolerance to the substance or use it to relieve withdrawal symptoms.

One of the most important aspects of dependence is that the substance use becomes a focal point of your day, often to the detriment of other activities or aspects of your life.

If established, once you have been dependent on a substance, it is very difficult then to reduce your use to small amounts or just occasionally. Usually, your use creeps up again towards the old established patterns. You may need some help to overcome your dependence, if it is longstanding. In some cases, you may need to have treatment for withdrawal symptoms as you begin to deal with your drug use. It's best to discuss this with your doctor.

Mental health problems and your decisions about substance use

Taking an illicit substance regularly or infrequently can interfere with your state of mind and mental health. When you have features of a mental health difficulty and take an illicit substance, in order to recover, you may need to decide to stop or at least reduce your use. This is the case if, despite receiving treatment for your depression or anxiety, you are not making progress.

Unravelling the connection between your substance use and depression

The way substance use and your mental health can interact can be very complex and change over time. The problem is that taking a substance will often, in some people, cause a short-lived state of mind which takes you away from the symptoms of depression or anxiety. The paradox is that there is generally a worsening of symptoms in the long run.

For many people who take a substance regularly, their mental health improves gradually and markedly once they stop their intake. In these cases, treatments used for depression and anxiety difficulties are unlikely to be very effective if substance use is ongoing or resumes. For some people, they commenced drug use when they became depressed or anxious, but the substance use then developed a life of its own. In these instances, a plan to deal with both is needed. This is possible. Treatments for depression and anxiety can help. Ongoing substance intake can interfere with medical and psychological treatments for depression and anxiety.

Some people assume that you cannot treat one problem until the other is resolved. This is not the case. You can address both at the same time, however, how much progress you make with either your substance problem or mental health problem depends on the relationship between them.

Tackling both elements of your problem

If you are dependent on a particular substance, you will need to decide on your goal with regards to your substance intake. Generally and overall, the best outcomes are achieved if you can aim to stop your use altogether.

Substance use is likely to make mental health problems worse. Until you can stop your substance use, you will need to make sure that you are safe when you use, particularly if you have been experiencing severe mental health problems. Some ways to do this include:

- do not use alone
- use smaller quantities
- do not mix with medications
- take precautions if you intend to use and are already feeling depressed or potentially suicidal
- tell someone you are using.

When you want to receive treatment for both problems from a health professional, this can be more challenging than if you had only one problem. This is because services such as mental health and drug and alcohol services are generally arranged to focus on one problem and not the other. General Practitioners are more used to seeing people with a combination of problems and are probably the best place to start for help.

Availability of illicit substances in rural and remote communities

There is a range of illicit substances that are available and being used in rural and remote communities. Some of the drugs mentioned in this section are generally common, such as cannabis and amphetamines. Other drugs like heroin and cocaine are less frequently marketed beyond the major urban centres. When and where particular drugs are available varies considerably. But it is reasonable to assume that even the most remote communities are affected by illicit substance use.

Illicit substances: known effects on mental health

In this section, only the potential effects of illicit substances on *mental* health are mentioned. It is important to note that the effects on *physical* health of some illicit drugs can be very serious – in some cases leading to death.

The effects of illicit drug use vary according to the potency of the substance, the amount taken, frequency of use, and the physical and health characteristics of the user.

The following descriptions are a basic guide only.

More detailed information about illicit drugs is available on the internet at www.druginfo.adf.org.au

Cannabis/Marijuana

Cannabis is the most widely-used illicit drug. It comes from the hemp plant, and is usually smoked (sometimes mixed with tobacco) or mixed with food like 'hash cookies'. Dependence (addiction) can occur with cannabis, even though there are no physical symptoms on withdrawal. Withdrawal symptoms can be prolonged, over several weeks, and include anxiety, an unpleasant, irritable, unhappy mood and agitation.

Known potential effects of cannabis/marijuana

These can arise during use, in intoxication and between episodes of use. Ongoing symptoms such as depression are more likely if there is regular weekly use.

Symptoms include:

- Confusion
- Anxiety – is one of the most common unwanted effects of use
- Panic
- Impaired memory and learning
- Paranoia and suspiciousness
- Aggressiveness
- Depressive symptoms (such as loss of interest and motivation, withdrawal, lowered libido and lethargy)
- Psychosis – which may include one or more of the following:
  - auditory hallucinations – hearing voices that aren't there
  - visual hallucinations – seeing things that aren't there
  - delusions – believing things that aren't true
  - jumbled thoughts and strange behaviour.
- As well as causing these symptoms of mental health difficulty, cannabis use can actually trigger depression, anxiety and schizophrenia in people who are vulnerable to developing them. The biggest risk of this is early in life during adolescence or early adulthood.

Amphetamines

Amphetamine-related drugs are widely available and are often called *speed*. Illicit drugs from this group include amphetamines, methamphetamine and methylenedioxymethamphetamine – *ecstasy*.

The most commonly abused amphetamine in Australia is methamphetamine which comes in different forms: tablets or capsules, crystals (often called *ice*) or a white, yellow or brown powder (more likely to be called *speed*) or paste (sometimes known as *base*).

Methods of use include swallowing, sniffing (the powder), injecting and (with the crystalline preparation) smoking. Most illegal methamphetamines are manufactured in makeshift laboratories and 'cut' (diluted) with different substances to boost profits. This means the person using the drug has no idea if the dose is strong or weak, or whether it contains other dangerous fillers. Some methamphetamines are smuggled into Australia from overseas. Users can become dependent on amphetamines. When this occurs, they are almost certain to notice some or many of the symptoms of mental health difficulties listed below.

Known potential effects of amphetamines

Acute intoxication generally leads to elevation of mood, insomnia and in some, agitation. It depends on whether you are a regular user or infrequent user and the dose taken. Symptoms of depression, insomnia and anxiety are often seen during the 'crash' phase after a period of use and are often mistaken for an episode of clinical depression.

It is more common for stimulant users to identify their mental health symptoms as problems and seek help for them, rather than to seek help for their substance use. It is worth remembering that many of the mental health problems experienced by regular amphetamine users will resolve when they stop their stimulant use.

Potential effects on mental health include:

- Depression, anxiety and related health difficulties
- Changeable mood
- Restlessness and agitation
- Insomnia
- Abnormal excitement and talkativeness
- Paranoia
- Aggressiveness
- Psychosis – which may include one or more of the following:
    - auditory hallucinations – hearing voices that aren't there
    - visual hallucinations – seeing things that aren't there
    - delusions – believing things that aren't true
    - jumbled thoughts and strange behaviour.
- Heavy, prolonged use causes brain damage to parts of the brain concerned with refined movement and executive brain functioning such as making complex plans and organisational ability.

- In addition to these effects, use can act as a trigger to the onset of a mental health difficulty such as depression, anxiety disorders or psychotic illnesses in people who are vulnerable.

Ice

Ice is a stimulant drug which has the effect of speeding up the messages travelling between the brain and the body. It is a type of methamphetamine which is generally stronger and more addictive with more harmful side effects than the powder form known as speed.

Ice usually takes the form of small chunky clear crystals that look like ice. It can also come as white or brownish crystal-like powder with a strong smell and bitter taste. It is also known as crystal meth, shabu, crystal, glass, shard, and P.

Ice is generally smoked or injected with its effects being felt in 3 to 7 seconds. It is also sometimes swallowed (taking effect after 15-30 minutes) or snorted (with effects occurring within 3-5 minutes).

Users of ice can quickly become dependent, and with higher doses of the drug put themselves at risk of heart attack, stroke, kidney disease, breathing difficulties, and even unconsciousness and death.

Known potential effects of ice

The effects of ice on mental health are now well documented and may include:

- Difficulties of concentration and sleep
- Agitation and confusion
- Anxiety
- Depression
- Paranoia

High doses of ice and frequent use may cause 'ice psychosis'. This is a condition characterised by paranoid delusions, hallucinations and bizarre, aggressive or violent behaviour.

Ecstasy

Ecstasy is a synthetic drug which acts as both a stimulant and hallucinogen, having the effect of speeding up the workings of the central nervous system and altering the users' perception of reality. It is commonly used at parties and nightclubs, and is most commonly available in the form of tablets.

Known potential effects of ecstasy
- Confusion
- Depression
- Anxiety
- Paranoia
- Insomnia
- Psychotic symptoms such as hallucinations (seeing things or hearing voices)

Cocaine

Cocaine refers to the drug in both a powder (cocaine) and crystal (crack) form that is derived from the coca plant. It is snorted as a powder, converted into a liquid for injecting, or in its crystal form, is smoked. This is a highly-addictive and dangerous drug. Users experience a short-lived high that is immediately followed by intense feelings of depression and a craving for more of the drug. People can develop dependence on cocaine.

Known potential effects of cocaine
- Depression
- Anxiety
- Anger and hostility
- Paranoia
- Insomnia
- Hallucinations (seeing things or hearing voices that aren't there)
- Ongoing mood disturbance

Opioids e.g. heroin

Heroin is an opioid derived from morphine or codeine, which are chemicals found in the milk of the opium poppy. It is available in the form of a powder which is white to brown in colour. It can be smoked, snorted/sniffed, but is usually injected. Street heroin is often mixed with other dangerous substances. Although heroin is the most recognised drug of abuse from this class of drugs, people often substitute other opioids for heroin when it is not available.

Most other opioids that are abused are prescribed drugs which are diverted from people receiving prescriptions into the black market or obtained illegally. They include methadone and buprenorphine (both are legitimately prescribed for heroin substitution programs and for pain), as well as codeine, morphine, pethidine and other similar medications. Some people only abuse prescribed opioids and they can experience the same range of difficulties as people taking heroin. Dependence on opioids is a serious problem. It can cause very unpleasant physical withdrawal effects when the drug is stopped abruptly which may require medication to manage.

Known potential effects of opioids

- Depression
- Dulled responses
- Poor concentration
- Anxiety
- Panic episodes

Solvents

Solvents are volatile substances with fumes that users deliberately inhale (often using a plastic bag). Some of the effects are similar to alcohol, except that they usually diminish more quickly than alcohol. Inhaling the fumes of solvents can be very dangerous to mental and physical health. Although these substances are not illicit for adults, because they are frequently used by adolescents and children, their sale to minors is prohibited in many communities.

Some of the products which may be sniffed include:

- Cigarette lighter refills (butane gas)
- Aerosols (where it is the propellant, often butane, which is inhaled)
- Solvent-based adhesives (some glues)
- Petrol
- Pressure pack spray paint.

Known potential effects of solvents

- Impaired mental activity
- Decreased self-control
- Disorientation/confusion
- Hallucinations (seeing things or hearing voices that aren't there)
- Delusions (believing things that aren't true)
- Brain damage, particularly impairment to the parts of the brain responsible for memory and executive brain functions such as controlling impulses.

CONFIDENTIAL OPTIONS FOR OBTAINING INFORMATION, COUNSELLING, REFERRAL AND TREATMENT

For information about substances/drugs	Want to contact a local drug and alcohol outreach service?
Want help to cut down or stop your use?	Need advice about or help with withdrawal?
Speak to your doctor	Speak to your doctor

NEED URGENT HELP?

Feel unsafe, out of control, highly restless or agitated, suicidal, or like you could explode and do someone harm?

Find the safest way of getting to the **Accident and emergency Department** of your nearest **Hospital** (like asking a relative, friend or neighbour to take you).

Where there is an issue of danger or safety as a result of drug use, there is also the option of calling an **Ambulance** by dialling 000

For help and support call 1300 85 85 84 or visit: Drug Info at www.druginfo.adf.org.au for a full list of national and local services or Counselling Online at www.counsellingonline.org.au to communicate with a professional counsellor about an alcohol or drug-related concern.

FOR HELP WITH?

- Understanding the effects of withdrawal
- Problems of addiction to prescribed drugs (like sedatives, tranquillisers or pain medication)
- Understanding the effects of misusing prescribed medication – or illegally or inappropriately obtained prescription medication
- Concerns about drug interactions (mixed illicit drugs, or prescription drugs with illicit drugs)

Speak to your doctor

For help and support call 1300 85 85 84 or visit: Drug Info at www.druginfo.adf.org.au for a full list of national and local services or Counselling Online at www.counsellingonline.org.au to communicate with a professional counsellor about an alcohol or drug-related concern.

WARNING SIGNS OF COMPLICATED GRIEF

Tick the signs that are familiar

Denial of feelings about the loss; no external signs of grieving – as if nothing had happened.

Being unable to talk fully about, acknowledge, or express the loss, or express feelings about it. Can't seem to be able to cry.

Unending, unchanging or prolonged distress, sadness, depression or guilt – still intensely preoccupied with the person who died

Acting out of character:
- with money, such as spending extravagantly
- by being sexually promiscuous
- making major changes in lifestyle or activities

Self-neglect: disinterest in personal appearance, eating properly or taking prescribed medication

Excessive use of alcohol or sedatives

Feeling agitated, restless, or manic

Prolonged lethargy, fatigue; noticeable physical and mental slowing down

Have become very absorbed in, and preoccupied with, helping and supporting others

Using work (working more than before and most of the time) or some other activity, as a way of keeping busy; 'getting on with things', in order not to have to feel the pain of grief

Unnerving fear (or phobia) about illness or death

Being careless, reckless, taking unnecessary risks (e.g. driving fast or dangerously)

Having thoughts about suicide, death, or self-harm

Feeling strong guilt about things other than actions taken or not taken at the time of the death

Have been functioning very poorly for a prolonged period

Strongly fixated on self-worthlessness

Hearing voices or seeing strange things other than hearing or momentarily seeing the deceased person.

If some of these signs or symptoms are familiar –

TAKE ACTION
Arrange to speak to a doctor

After medical assessment, you may be referred (or will need to request referral) to a grief therapist.

Having thoughts about suicide or self-harm are serious.
If you are having these thoughts –

TAKE URGENT ACTION
Arrange to speak to a doctor OR phone

PHONE A 24-HOUR MENTAL HEALTH EMERGENCY LINE

Lifeline: 13 11 14
Suicide Call Back Service: 1300 659 467

For help and support phone the GriefLine on 1300 845 745 or visit GriefLine Community and Family Services at www.griefline.org.au for a full list of services.

ABOUT GRIEF

Grief is the reaction we have to most significant losses in our lives. Some of the losses that commonly give rise to a grief reaction include:

- ending a relationship
- loss of career or employment
- death of a pet
- loss of a significant role or position of status
- loss of health
- loss of cherished plans, a goal or dream.

One of the most disturbing losses that all of us will be likely to experience is bereavement: the death of a person who is significant to us. Since bereavement often gives rise to a major grief reaction, what we observe of bereavement grief can help us to make sense of the grief of most other losses. Bereavement grief will be the focus of this section.

Bereavement Grief

The grief of bereavement is a reaction, psychologically and physically, to the changes thrust upon us because of a person's death. We are forced to find a different way of going about our lives, coping with the gaps, and a whole host of unforeseen changes and happenings.

How severely we experience grief, and for how long, depends on many factors such as: what the lost person meant to us – how significant the person was to our sense of well-being or security; how involved we were with the person; what role we played in caring for him/her (such as in the case of a long period of illness); how strongly we identified with the person's experience or that of others around him/her. Our state of mind, health, emotional resilience, and what other things were happening in our lives at the time, are also factors.

Bereavement is not only a major loss in itself, but it often sets off a chain reaction of other losses (that may also have to be grieved and adapted to) such as:

- loss of income or financial security/stability
- loss of routine, stability, and order promoted by (amongst other things) the demands of having to adopt new roles (perhaps once those of the deceased) and take on new tasks and responsibilities
- loss of a future together, or one in which the deceased would have played a significant role
- loss of home or accommodation arrangements
- loss of mutual friends
- loss of opportunities for social gatherings and interactions that were previously linked to the deceased person's work or interests.

Although its initial intensity usually diminishes with time, grief may be felt for an extended period, even up to several years. Sometimes, the pain of grief intensifies during the first few months after the death, because not only are the reality and consequences of the loss 'sinking in,' but the support of others tends to fall away – often because people less affected have moved on or, if similarly affected, are preoccupied with their own pain and struggle.

Grief is a journey that demands a lot of patience, effort, energy, and a preparedness to experience much emotion. As well, it calls for the courage and daring to walk a new path, and to adapt to new challenges with hopefulness.

Normal Grief

Normal grief encompasses a whole range of emotional and mental experiences, characterised by:

Shock – Feelings of numbness, unreality, emotional detachment, being in a dreamlike state, which may last for minutes, hours, or weeks.

Pain of grief – A very painful emotional/psychological anguish, with often considerable physical discomfort, including: shaking, wrenching of the gut, uncontrollable crying, chest pain, and weakness. This 'whole of person' anguish is what we term grief. Grief can be powerfully intense at first, only subsiding with the passing of time – but often able to be reactivated by reminders of the deceased.

A sense of loss – This is often the trigger for grief: realising at an emotional level that the one who has been lost cannot be retrieved. This is the experience of losing not only the person who has died, but also all of the things associated with the relationship, such as companionship, shared activities and responsibilities, communication, affection, future plans.

Anger – A common emotion associated with being or feeling powerless, losing one's sense of order, control; being unable to change or alter what has happened. Anger may be directed at others (because it often needs someone to blame) or at oneself.

Guilt – often mingled with regret and anger, may be felt for not being the person who died – for surviving; or because of some sense of responsibility for the death, for the degree of the deceased person's suffering, for not having been honest, available, loyal, caring enough – or perhaps insistent about that person's safety or health. ("Why didn't I make her stop smoking?")

Regrets – are common no matter how good a relationship was; regrets about things left undone or unsaid, or about missed opportunities – how things could have been.

Anxiety and fearfulness – are a response to life's order, predictability, security, and one's own sense of balance having been overturned. Being faced with such upheaval, and a keen sense of emotional vulnerability, can bring waves of acute anxiety and feelings of panic.

Intrusive images – These can occur particularly if the death happened in dramatic or traumatic circumstances, or where immense meaning was associated with the events of the death. Such images can be quite vivid and detailed, and may emerge most when one is alone, before going to sleep, or when one is mentally less active.

Mental disorganisation – In the early weeks of bereavement – and sometimes persisting for months – the experience of some mental disorganisation including poor concentration, confusion, forgetfulness, and being easily distracted, is common.

Feeling overwhelmed – The sometimes immense emotional and mental upheaval of loss and grief can be experienced as profoundly overwhelming – including for people who have always prided themselves on their ability to cope with adversity. Compromised in their usual capacity for thinking things through and maintaining emotional balance, they may nevertheless have to deal with a whole range of practical tasks and demands.

Relief – When a spouse, partner, relative, or friend has suffered a prolonged illness, or much pain, disfigurement, or personality change, it is quite normal to feel relief when they die – because of their suffering (and one's own feeling of being powerless to change the inevitable), or perhaps because of being fatigued by the great demands of devoted caring.

Loneliness – It is common, even in the company of caring and supportive relatives and friends, to feel very alone in grief. After several months of bereavement, a person may feel loneliness most severely. Other people (perhaps less close to or involved with the deceased) have moved on; their lives appear to be back to normal. The blurring and preoccupying pain and turmoil of grief begins to permit the realisation of aloneness in a new and stark way: the loss of companionship, sharing of intimacy, experiences, daily tasks and responsibilities. Particularly for the elderly, loneliness can be a profoundly diminishing and depressing experience.

Positive feelings – Grief does not prevent positive feelings and experiences altogether. Quite contrary to any idea of showing disrespect for the deceased, they may be a celebration of, and compliment to, the quality of a former relationship. That one can sometimes emerge out of grief and see the goodness of life, the future it holds, and experience some ordinary day-to-day things with joy and pleasure, is a sign of 'healthy' grief.

Grief Avoidance

No one wants to experience the pain and upheaval of grief. Who wouldn't want to avoid it? The problem is that it can only be avoided at our peril. It doesn't go away if ignored – if anything, it becomes even more overwhelming for having been delayed.

> **IMPORTANT**
>
> People who are grieving **will from time-to-time need to 'take a break'** or be distracted from the pain and emotion of grief. They will also need to pay attention to the new tasks, challenges, role demands, and practicalities created by bereavement (which will tend to prompt, on occasions, a return to experiencing grief emotion). Part of healthy coping with grief is when a person moves between the pain and emotion of loss and the tasks, challenges, and practicalities of 'restoration': attending to life changes, doing new things, forming a new identity and new relationships.

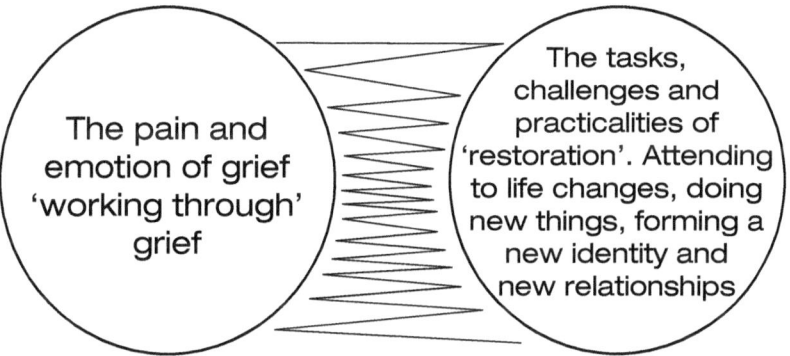

It is when these patterns become rigid, fixed, or are used excessively that they become a problem, because they supplant a normal process of grieving.

Seeking to avoid grief altogether is never helpful. Bereaved people commonly use one or more of a variety of *grief avoidance patterns* in a bid to escape dealing with grief. Some of these patterns are a quite legitimate, *temporary* means of survival and coping. People who use these patterns are usually unconscious or only partly conscious of doing so.

Continually avoiding grief means avoiding feelings, the capacity to enjoy life, living and loving; this results in moving away from oneself and others.

To deny, continually suppress, block, or deaden a grief experience can have serious consequences for:

- mental health
- physical health
- relationships
- personal safety
- future life.

Grief Avoidance Patterns	Potential Consequences
Postponing "I don't want to deal with it now… I've got too much else to do." This is fine as a temporary or occasional respite from grief.	When grieving is postponed for a prolonged period, it builds up inside and can become explosive. Postponing grieving by getting on with things is often reinforced by others who compliment the bereaved person for "doing very well." Sensing this build-up as unsafe, the bereaved person has further reason to postpone experiencing feelings related to the loss.
Misdirecting grief emotions By not acknowledging grief or not allowing the grieving process to occur properly, some people *misdirect* the emotional content of grief onto other issues or other people. Shifting the powerful emotions of grief away from their proper setting and source can cause confusion and real problems.	This can damage relationships, by exaggerating issues and problems. It can cause the person to become increasingly angry; to feel powerless, overwhelmed, or even under attack by others. Pressures of work and daily living can become flashpoints for reaction and defensiveness.
Replacing A quite common pattern, *replacing* describes when a person prematurely shifts the emotional focus that was	Grief does not go away by being ignored, or because some nurturing is experienced in a new relationship. It is a powerful force, and if ignored

Replacing *(continued)* once part of their relationship with the deceased onto a new relationship. This diverts attention away from the grief associated with the deceased; but only temporarily, and with often destructive consequences.	can be corrosive of the bereaved person's mental state and emotional stability, as well as undermining the new relationship – often spelling hurt and misunderstanding for both people.
Minimising The *minimiser* attempts to convince him/herself and others that he/she is coping really well and has not been overly affected by the loss. Avoiding pain at all costs, the minimiser deludes him/herself that 'thinking through' grief is the same as the necessary experiencing grief. There is a tendency to rationalise away the vital felt component of grief.	Trying to convince him/herself that grief has been overcome (which is often applauded by others as "coping really well"), the bereaved person becomes less able to engage with the emotion of grief, and sets him/herself up for being overwhelmed by it; which can contradict their former claims.
Overworking Again a very common avoidance pattern, *overworking* describes when a bereaved person over-invests in work as a way of leaving no time available to think or feel about the loss. Common advice by well-wishers is often, "Keep busy and occupy your mind."	Unfortunately, compulsively overworking to avoid the pain of grief usually results in more pain, once grief can no longer be avoided or organised out of the daily work schedule.

Retail therapy This avoidance pattern provides only very short-term relief from the necessity of grieving. Nevertheless, some people throw themselves into a disastrously unrestrained pattern of shopping. Some may rationalise this behaviour as "being kind to myself for once" or "doing something for me."	The consequence of this behaviour will, at best, be disappointment at its short-lived effect. At worst, it may create a whole new problem to add an unnecessary burden to grief: financial debt and guilt associated with it.
Overeating *Overeating* is well known to be a behaviour exhibited by emotionally deprived children: using something that is available, in some sense to compensate for a person (usually a relinquishing or absent parent) who is unavailable and yearned for. In bereavement, overeating may be an unconscious attempt to fill the emptiness – to compensate for the void created by loss. We also know that when people appear unable to acknowledge stress, hunger centres in the brain are stimulated.	Overeating is sometimes characterised by a compulsive craving for food, which a person may feel powerless to stop. The unfortunate consequences of overeating are the physical and psychological problems that result from weight gain.

Alcohol and drug use Alcohol and other drugs (including misused prescription drugs) are too often used to avoid the work of mourning loss. Well-meaning friends may suggest: "Here, take this, it will make you feel better."	This is one of the most dangerous of avoidance patterns because, though seeming to improve mood and sleep, and though very effective in temporarily blocking out memories, it is quite counter-productive. Using alcohol or drugs in this way may lead to significant problems of addiction and escalating dependence and abuse. Alcohol, as an example, rather than having benefits, may impair the quality of sleep, worsen mood and cause anxiety and agitation. Chemical abuse, as a means of avoiding the pain and process of grieving, may easily become a more generalised pattern of behaviour for years to come.
Moving away Some people who are bereaved seek to avoid the process and work of mourning by staying on the move, travelling, or prematurely changing their place of residence. This may be prompted by a well-meaning friend advising: "What you need is to get away from it all."	To move away from a familiar environment, social support, and the 'prompts' so useful to maintaining progress in the mourning process, may simply delay and intensify the inevitable accommodation of grief. Leaving what is familiar and supportive can also create secondary losses that further add to the upheaval of grief.

Crusading	Premature involvement in a cause, albeit a very good one, can inhibit and delay the necessary work of mourning, and may cause 'loss of face,' guilt and regret at letting others down, when grief overwhelmingly demands attention.
Crusading is becoming prematurely involved in or committed to a cause. It is probably quite true to say that we can, "help ourselves by helping others," but not if this is a premature distraction from the necessary work of mourning. It is all too easy to get passionately involved in voluntary work, like setting up a fundraising campaign for cancer research or a hospice, or throwing oneself into some other just cause, as a way of unknowingly trying to postpone the task of grieving.	

MEN AND WOMEN GRIEVE DIFFERENTLY

People will grieve in their own particular and individual way. It is important as well, to recognise that men and women tend to grieve differently. We are probably most familiar with how women grieve, because they tend to do so more publicly than men. But if men are to be adequately and appropriately supported, we need to understand how their way of grieving often differs from that of women.

Women and grief

Women are usually very good at seeking out support for themselves and supporting each other. They tend to relieve their emotional pain through open expression of it, and talking about it in the company of others. When women encounter difficulties with grieving, it is usually not because they don't accommodate the emotional experience of grief, but because they pay too little attention to the tasks, challenges, and practicalities of restoration: attending to life changes, doing new things, forming a new identity and new relationships.

Men and grief

Contrary to the popular view that men do not cope as well with bereavement and grief as women, research suggests that only when men are deprived of social support do they fare more poorly than women. But what is important to note, in comparing men and women, is that they exhibit differences in *their way* of grieving, and not just by choice, but because of differences in biology (brain functions and structure, and hormonal systems) and in society-reinforced roles.

How men tend to respond to grief

- Men are not as self-caring or help-seeking as women.
- Men pay less attention to emotional pain than women, until those around them appear 'safe' and things appear 'in order.' This is because men often distance themselves from the emotional content of difficult or 'threatening' situations in order to remain vigilant and protective towards others.
- Men tend to need more time and have to make more of a conscious effort to connect with grief emotions.

- Men often need privacy, aloneness, or a 'safe' ritual place (like a cemetery), before facing and experiencing emotional pain.
- Men are generally much less verbal than women, preferring to 'mull things over' and think things through.
- Men tend to exhibit more anger than women. This can pose a problem for men, because people tend to be sympathetic to the more subtle emotions that women exhibit, and unsympathetic to men whose dominant emotion is often anger. Unfortunately, what is not realised is that behind anger there are usually all the subtle emotions (like sadness, yearning, and helplessness) and suffering, just as others are experiencing, but in different order of presentation.
- Men often respond negatively to pressure to be more public in their grieving than they feel comfortable with.
- Men usually achieve through activities, action, small rituals (connected to their grief), and 'mulling things over,' what women do by talking and 'crying out' their grief.
- Men benefit much from the company of other men (or working alongside other men); not necessarily by any verbal exchange, but just by another man being 'present' who cares, but doesn't intrude.

How grieving men can best help themselves

- By showing courage in allowing themselves to experience the painful emotions of grief (rather than continuing to push them underground)
- By communicating clearly to others their need to be alone and to deal with their feelings in private
- By not shutting others out, but keeping communication open in their relationships
- By 'tuning in' to their bodies (Some feelings can be expressed as physical health problems.)
- By consciously using rituals and activity through which to express and work with their grief
- By slowing down, and making time for being reflective, and to connect with their grief (making time to grieve in order for there to be time to heal)
- By staying close to reliable friends and talking to them

- By taking time out in the natural environment (away from work), to be open, vulnerable, and reflective

Coping with Grief

The emotional pain and internal upheaval that many people experience following a death can feel almost unbearable. Thankfully, the pain does ease with time, and some sense of internal order can be felt returning. But grief is not just feelings, it is a complex process of reaction to loss, adjustment to the absence of the deceased (with the many challenges that may create), and an endeavour to make sense of what has happened, what it means, and what it implies about the future.

Grief mostly resolves, and life, though never being quite the same (because some things have changed forever), finds a new order and balance, permitting hope and promoting again the experience of pleasure and the possibility of human happiness.

If this were not so, how would past generations have survived the grief of war, holocaust, disasters, and disease?

Though there are many factors that determine the course of grief and how well an individual copes and adapts, as with physical healing, there are many simple strategies and measures that can help to heal the grief of bereavement:

- Getting some time to yourself each day is important for reflection, and to allow the experience of emotions, perhaps put on hold during the day. To avoid being interrupted, you may need to turn off your mobile phone or go somewhere where you won't be disturbed.
- Try writing down (in a private diary or exercise book) your thoughts of the day. Putting them where they can be seen may help you in making sense of them or just keeping them in proportion. Doing this (throughout the grieving process) can provide you with visual proof of your progress; this will be something you can come back to and be reassured by when you're having a difficult day or feel discouraged. It may also (in addition to thoughts) be helpful to make note of the different kinds of feelings you are experiencing and their intensity.
- Make an extra effort to spend time with other supportive people – especially when you least feel like it or are having a difficult day. Interacting with other people can be very helpful in giving your mood a lift.

- Having a good cry can leave you feeling a whole lot better, and is an important step in the healing process. It may be necessary to find a place where you can do this, where you are sure you won't be seen or heard. It will be well worth the effort.
- Avoid making any major decisions, at least (if possible) for the first year of bereavement.
- Try to take life one day at a time; don't think too far ahead and, when difficult problems come up that have to be dealt with, try using the Structured Problem-Solving method to help.
- One of the most difficult issues to think clearly about and to deal with when you are grieving is finances. It is in this circumstance that you can most justify and benefit from the assistance of a financial advisor, accountant or rural counsellor. No one wants to make their business known to others, but some occasions, like bereavement, need to be an exception.
- Talk about the person who has died with other people – especially those who knew him/her. Though this may be quite uncomfortable at first, it can increasingly diminish the pain of grief and the power of the whole situation to feel so wounding.
- Find someone you feel comfortable confiding in and who is a good listener. You may need to ask your doctor or your nearest Community Health Service to recommend someone who has specialist grief counselling training.

Remember, even if your first experience of speaking to someone like this doesn't work out, don't give up; try to find someone else, because they may prove to be a vital lifeline. A grief counsellor will normally be trained to help you cope with and make sense of the experience, emotional adjustments, and tasks of grieving. Some of these include:
- the need to accept the reality of the loss
- working through and allowing for the experience of emotional pain
- adjusting to the physical absence of the deceased
- finding a new and enduring place for the deceased in your life; such as finding ways to remember the person so that he/she remains 'present' and continues to be valued, whilst still allowing for life to go on and progress.

- Write letters to the person you have lost, expressing your feelings and thoughts. Read them at the person's graveside, keep them in a

safe place, or maybe put them under a tree or bush planted in his/her memory.
- Create a memorial for the person who died: plant a tree, build something in the garden, compile a photo album, or create a mementos box with significant things in it.
- Commemorate the person on special days (on birthdays, Christmas, anniversaries or other significant occasions): light a candle, eat or drink something that the person liked, put their photograph out in pride of place.

TAKING CARE OF YOURSELF

- Try to get into a regular daily routine with set times for getting up, eating meals, and going to bed.
- Avoid trying to feel better or covering over your grief through alcohol, smoking, medication, or other drugs.
- Avoid too much coffee or tea, and other drinks that have caffeine in them (like cola), because they can make getting to sleep more difficult and can worsen any tendency to be anxious.
- Get yourself relaxed well prior to bedtime to improve getting to sleep.
- Do some outdoor activities (preferably not associated with work) like walking or gardening – to refresh you mentally.
- Try to achieve a balanced diet, including: breads, cereals, lean meat, fish, lots of vegetables, fruit, and some dairy products.
- Find ways of regularly relaxing. Use especially relaxing music, a relaxation tape, meditation, or some other proven method of relaxation.
- Get regular daily exercise to help your mood and general sense of well-being. It doesn't need to be strenuous. If you are concerned about physical health problems, or haven't had a medical check-up lately, make an appointment to see a doctor.
- Give yourself permission to take a break from grief sometimes and do something enjoyable and pleasurable.

HELPING SOMEONE ELSE COPE WITH GRIEF

Although we may feel awkward and blundering in our attempt to support someone who is bereaved, so long as we are genuine, and are not using the situation to explore or grapple with our own feelings or issues, then our efforts may prove really helpful for them. How well a person copes with grief depends significantly on the quality of support they receive from others.

The following suggestions are a basic guide for helping someone else to cope with grief.

Things to do
- Provide practical assistance. Often more than anything else, a bereaved person appreciates help with practical things such as work-related tasks and responsibilities (for those living on a farm, this may include mending a fence, getting a tractor in for repair, dealing with stock issues), childcare, bill paying, mowing a lawn, domestic chores or cooking. It may ring hollow to wish a person well if what they are most needful of is practical help.
- Don't be afraid to visit and ask how they are, or to mention the deceased.
- Maintain contact, preferably in person, but also consider phoning, or sending a note or card. Support is often needed most once all the initial activity has subsided (after the funeral), and numbness gives way to raw painful emotion (sometimes persisting for several months).
- Talk about the person who has died using straight-forward language.
- Be aware of particular dates, anniversaries or times of the year that might be upsetting to the bereaved. Be available, call in and see them, telephone or send a card, to indicate your care and support.
- Try your best to be a good listener: maintain concentration, be patient, and show by your body language, eye contact, and attentiveness, that you are interested.
- Accept their behaviour (unless it is unsafe) and their ways of dealing with the emotional pain of grief. Allow for emotion, expressions of blame, guilt, anger, and regret. Just let it be; just be present.
- If it seems appropriate and needed, offer the comments (not advice) that:

- Grief takes time (just like a physical wound that is painful before healing).
- Everyone grieves in their own way and in their own time.

Things to be aware of:
- Respect the dignity and independence of the bereaved person. Put yourself in their shoes and imagine: "How would I feel in these circumstances – being spoken to like this?"
- Avoid giving advice, but if a matter of safety is involved, tell the person clearly what your concerns are.
- Before you offer support, decide what your commitment will be. It is most unhelpful to withdraw your support along the way because you're not really committed or because you find their emotions too uncomfortable.
- Avoid using clichés or platitudes; these most often come across as insincere and patronising.
- Don't give false assurances or talk a lot because the situation feels awkward for you.
- Try not to talk about yourself, your own problems, or your own grief, unless you are asked and, even then, be sparing in what you say.
- Don't say: "I know how you feel." How you felt in *similar* circumstances was not exactly the same.
- Avoid lecturing or imparting theory about grief. You could give the person something to read on grief if you think he/she would be receptive to that.
- Don't take over, and don't 'rescue.' The last thing a person needs is to have to expend energy on avoiding unwanted help, or figuring out how to tell a well-meaning rescuer to leave them be!
- Avoid suggesting any time frame about the duration of the person's grief.
- Be conscious of not shifting the focus away from the bereaved person because what they are saying is tedious, uninteresting, or uncomfortable. Although the content of what the person says may be repetitious and full of familiar emotion, he/she may be helped considerably by being able to express it to someone they trust.
- Don't trivialise their grief ("everybody experiences grief").
- Don't catastrophise their grief ("It's a terrible thing... some people never get over it").

Structured Problem-Solving

For people who are bereaved, feeling stressed and overwhelmed by problems is common. Adopting a new way of tackling problems can be very helpful.

Structured problem-solving is a method designed to help you feel in control of your problems, and to enable you to deal more effectively with future problems.

The **key elements** of this method include:

- identifying and 'pinning down' the problems that have contributed to you feeling overwhelmed
- thinking clearly and constructively about problems
- 'taking stock' of how you've coped in the past: your personal strengths, and the support and resources available to you
- providing a sound basis for important decision-making.

With this method you can work on a single problem or follow the process to tackle a number of problems.

Usually though – especially to begin with – it is best to deal with one problem that is specific and potentially solvable.

STRUCTURED PROBLEM-SOLVING INVOLVES 6 STEPS

Step 1
Write down the problem causing you worry or distress:

Step 2
Think about your options for dealing with this problem (try to think broadly – including good and not so good options); write them down:

1.	
2.	
3.	
4.	
5.	

Step 3

Write down the advantages and disadvantages of each option:

Step 4

Identify the best option(s) to deal with the problem:

1.	
2.	
3.	
4.	
5.	

STEP 5

List the steps needed to carry out each option (bear in mind the resources needed and pitfalls to overcome):

1. a.
b.
c.
2. a.
b.
c.
3. a.
b.
c.
4. a.
b.
c.
5. a.
b.
c.

STEP 6

Review your progress in carrying out your option(s):

What have I achieved? ....

....

What still needs to be done? ....

....

RESTORING A NORMAL PATTERN OF SLEEP

Sleep disturbance is common for those experiencing grief, and frequently takes the form of early-morning wakening (usually around 3am) with difficulty returning to sleep. To restore a normal pattern of sleep, it's important to practise sleep-promoting behaviour during the day, in the evening, at bedtime, and during the night.

Better Sleep Guidelines

During the Day

- Organise your day. Regular times for eating meals, taking medicines, performing chores and other activities, help keep our inner clocks running smoothly.
- Regular exercise during the day (or early evening) can improve sleeping patterns.
- Set aside time for problem-solving and decision-making during the day, to avoid worry or anxiety at night.
- Avoid napping during the day, go to bed and get up at regular times.

During the Evening

- Put the day to rest. If you still have things on your mind, write them down or put them in your Daily Activities Diary, to be dealt with tomorrow.
- Light exercise early in the evening may help sleep. Avoid exercise late in the evening, as this may make getting to sleep more difficult.
- Get into a routine of 'winding down' during the course of the evening, allowing at least half an hour of quiet activity, such as reading or listening to music, prior to bedtime.
- Avoid drinking caffeinated drinks after about 4pm, and don't drink more than 2 cups of caffeinated drinks each day (especially coffee, tea, cocoa, and cola).
- Avoid smoking for at least an hour (preferably an hour and a half) before going to bed.
- Don't use alcohol to make you sleep, and keep your intake moderate (limit yourself to 2 standard drinks each day). Have 1 or 2 alcohol-free days each week.

- Make sure your bed and bedroom are comfortable – not too cold or too warm.
- Ensure that your bedroom is dark and that the morning light does not filter in. However, if you have a tendency to oversleep, it may be helpful to let the morning light into the room.
- Avoid a heavy meal close to bedtime. If you are hungry, a light snack may help you get to sleep.

At Bedtime

- Try to do the same things before you go to bed each night.
  Develop a calming bedtime routine, such as having a warm bath or shower, listening to relaxation music, or using a relaxation technique. This way your body will learn to know that (with these activities) you are getting ready to go to sleep.
- Go to bed when you feel 'sleepy tired' and not before.
- Don't watch TV or have conversations or arguments in bed. Keep your bed and bedroom only for sleep (and sexual activity).
- Turn the light off when you get into bed.
- Relax and tell yourself that sleep will come when it is ready.
  Enjoy relaxing your mind and body, even if you don't fall asleep at first.

During the Night

- If you wake up too early in the night, don't lie awake for more than 30 minutes. Instead of just being awake or worrying, get out of bed and do something that is distracting yet relaxing. Return to bed only when you feel sleepy again.
- Get up at the same time each morning. Don't sleep late in the morning trying to make up for 'lost sleep.'
- If you live in a place or area where there are sounds or noises that might wake you from sleep, use earplugs to block out the noise.
- Avoid sleeping pills – they do not provide a long-term solution to sleep problems.

KEY SERVICES AND RESOURCES

When you call a crisis or information and referral number, you should expect a similar response from each type of service.

1. **Information and Referral services**

    The phone will be answered by a trained operator who will:
    - Listen to you
    - Provide support by:
    – Offering advice and helping you find information
    – Suggesting services that will be helpful including medical, psychological and support services in your local area
    – Referring you to a crisis service if necessary (e.g. Lifeline)
    – Contacting a crisis service on your behalf if necessary.

2. **Crisis services**

    The phone will be answered by a professional who will:
    - Discuss your problems and provide information
    - Provide an assessment and counselling (if needed)
    - Provide support and counselling during a period of crisis
    - Provide clear psychiatric information
    - Provide referral to a service/person to assist you with ongoing care if needed including:
    – Specialist psychiatric service
    – Mental health team
    – General practitioner (GP)
    – Local support services.

NATIONAL

Lifeline 13 11 14
24 hours a day, 7 days a week
Confidential telephone counselling.

SANE Australia helpline 1800 187 263
9am–5pm, Monday to Friday
Information and referral about mental health issues.

Kids Help Line 1800 55 1800
24 hours a day, 7 days a week
Free and confidential telephone and online counselling service for young people aged between 5 and 25.

Suicide Call Back Service 1300 659 467

Carers Australia 1800 242 636

Relationships Australia 1300 364 277

Post and Antenatal Depression Association (PANDA) 1300 726 306

GriefLine 1300 845 745

Cannabis Information and Helpline 1800 30 40 50
11am–7pm, Monday to Friday (including public holidays)

Family Drug Help 1300 660 068
24 hours a day, 7 days a week

Family Drug Support 1300 368 186
24 hours a day, 7 days a week
Support for families faced with problematic drug use.

Quitline 13 78 48
8am–8pm, Monday to Friday

Adverse Medicine Events Line 1300 134 237
9am to 5pm, Monday to Friday (excluding NSW public holidays)
Not for emergencies. Report and discuss adverse experiences with your medications.

Medicines Line 1300 MEDICINE OR 1300 633 424
9am to 5pm, Monday to Friday (excluding NSW public holidays)
Information on prescription, over-the-counter and complementary (herbal, 'natural', vitamin and mineral) medicines.

STATE AND TERRITORY SERVICES

VICTORIA
Mental Health Advice Line 1800 280 737
SuicideLine 1300 651 251
Parenting Line 13 22 89
DirectLine 1800 888 236
24 hours a day, 7 days a week
Confidential alcohol and drug counselling and referral line.
1800 ICE ADVICE 1800 423 238
24 hours a day, 7 days a week – Advice and support for people who use ice, their families and health professionals.
Pharmacotherapy, Advocacy, Mediation & Support (PAMS)
1800 443 844
10am–6pm, Monday to Friday
Advice for anyone experiencing trouble with their pharmacotherapy program (Methadone, Suboxone etc.).
Youth Drug and Alcohol Advice (YoDAA) Line 1800 458 685
9am–8pm, Monday to Friday
Telephone information and advice for young people and others concerned about them.

NEW SOUTH WALES
Salvo Suicide Prevention and Crisis Line
Metro: 02 9331 2000
Rural: 1300 363 622
Parentline: 1300 1300 52
Alcohol and Drug Information Service (ADIS)
Sydney: 02 9361 8000 Regional NSW: 1800 422 599
A 24-hour confidential information, advice and referral telephone service.
Ted Noffs Foundation help line
NSW/ACT: 1800 151 045
24 hours a day, 7 days a week
Counselling and support for young people and their families.
NSW Mental Health Line
1800 011 511
24 hours a day, 7 days a week connecting you with the right care

QUEENSLAND

Salvo Suicide Prevention and Crisis Line
Metro: 07 3831 9016
Rural: 1300 363 622
Parentline: 1300 30 1300

Alcohol and Drug Information Service (ADIS)
1800 177 833
24-hour Alcohol and Drug Information Service
Telephone information, counselling and referral.

WESTERN AUSTRALIA

Mental Health Emergency Response Line
Metro: 1300 555 788
Rural: 1800 552 002
Parentline: 1800 654 432

Parent Drug Information Service (PDIS)
Perth: 08 9442 5050
Regional: 1800 653 203

Alcohol & Drug Information Service (ADIS)
Perth: 08 9442 5000
Regional WA: 1800 198 024
A 24-hour, confidential telephone service that provides information, counselling, referral and advice.

SOUTH AUSTRALIA

Mental Health Assessment and Crisis Intervention Service
13 14 65

Parentline 1300 364 100

Alcohol and Drug Information Service (ADIS)
1300 131 340
24-hours, 7 days a week
Telephone information, counselling, and referral service.

AUSTRALIAN CAPITAL TERRITORY

Crisis Assessment and Treatment Team: 1800 629 354
Parentline: 1300 1300 52

AUSTRALIAN CAPITAL TERRITORY continued

Alcohol and Drug Information Service (ADIS)
02 6207 9977
24-hour telephone service offering information, advice, referral, intake, assessment and support.

TASMANIA

Mental Health Services Helpline: 1800 332 388

Parenting Line: 1300 808 178

Alcohol and Drug Information Service (ADIS)
1800 811 994
A 24-hour telephone information and counselling line.

NORTHERN TERRITORY

Mental Health On Call Team
Top End: 08 8999 4988
Central Australia: 08 8951 7710
Parentline: 1300 30 1300

Alcohol and Drug Information Service (ADIS)
1800 131 350
24-hour Alcohol and Drug Telephone Information and counselling service.

ABORIGINAL AND TORRES STRAIT ISLANDER INFORMATION

If you are an Aboriginal or Torres Strait Islander person reading this book or if you are concerned about an Aboriginal or Torres Strait Islander person, contact your local Aboriginal health service. The following can put you in touch with a range of support services including *Bringing Them Home* counsellors, information on *Link Up* services and other counselling options:

Office for Aboriginal and Torres Strait Islander Health (OATSIH)
www.health.gov.au/oatsih

National Aboriginal Community Controlled Health Organisation (NACCHO) www.naccho.org.au
Links to Aboriginal Community Controlled Health Services and Aboriginal Medical Services in each state and territory

Australian Indigenous Health *InfoNet*
www.healthinfonet.ecu.edu.au
Information about Indigenous health, including detailed overviews of specific health topics

Australian Indigenous Mental Health
http://indigenous.ranzcp.org
Training modules to support mental health professionals throughout Australia in their work with Aboriginal and Torres Strait Islander people

NATIONAL WEBSITES

Anxiety Network Australia www.anxietynetwork.com.au
Information about anxiety disorders and self-help programs

Australian Drug Foundation www.adf.org.au
Information on alcohol and drugs and on problems arising from their misuse

beyondblue www.beyondblue.org.au
Information on depression, anxiety and related disorders, available treatments and where to get help

Black Dog Institute www.blackdoginstitute.org.au
Information about bipolar disorder and depression

Bluepages www.bluepages.anu.edu.au
Information about depression and treatments

Carers Australia www.carersaustralia.com.au
Family carer support and counselling in each state and territory

Counselling Online www.counsellingonline.org.au
Free, online professional drug and alcohol counselling

CRUfAD (Clinical Research Unit for Anxiety and Depression) www.crufad.org
Information and internet-based education and treatment programs for people with depression and anxiety

depressionservices.org.au www.depressionservices.org.au
Information, support and online counselling for Australians living with depression

e-couch www.ecouch.anu.edu.au
Online counselling service which provides information about emotional problems, including depression and anxiety disorders, and strategies to help prevent and manage problems

headspace – Australia's National Youth Mental Health Foundation www.headspace.org.au
Information, support and help for young people aged between 12 and 25

HealthInsite www.healthinsite.gov.au
A wide range of up-to-date information on health topics such as diabetes, cancer, mental health and asthma

Kids Helpline www.kidshelp.com.au
Web, email and telephone counselling for children and young people aged between 5 and 25

Mental Illness Fellowship of Australia Inc
www.mifellowshipaustralia.org.au
Information, support and advocacy for people with serious mental illnesses, their families and friends

MoodGym www.moodgym.anu.edu.au
Free online Cognitive Behaviour Therapy program designed to prevent depression in young adults

Multicultural Mental Health Australia (MMHA)
www.mmha.org.au
Information about the mental health and well-being of Australians from culturally and linguistically diverse backgrounds, including Fact sheets in languages other than English

PANDA (Post and Antenatal Depression Association)
www.panda.org.au
Information, telephone helpline and referral to anyone affected by post and antenatal depression, including partners and extended family

Parentline www.parentline.com.au
Parentline is a confidential telephone counselling service aimed at providing professional counselling and support for parents and others who care for children.

RANZCP consumer information www.ranzcp.org/resources/clinical-practice-guidelines.html
The Royal Australian and New Zealand College of Psychiatrists site contains psychiatric clinical guidelines and a series of Treatment Guides

for consumers and carers available on the following topics: Anorexia Nervosa; Bipolar Disorder; Deliberate Self Harm; Depression; Panic Disorder and Agoraphobia; Schizophrenia.

ReachOut.com www.reachout.com
Information to help young people through tough times

Relationships Australia www.relationships.com.au
Support and counselling for relationships

SANE Australia www.sane.org
Information about mental illness symptoms, treatments, where to go for support and help for carers

Suicide Call Back Service www.suicidecallbackservice.org.au
Online resources and telephone support and for those at risk of suicide, their carers and those bereaved by suicide

Sources Used in the Preparation of this Book

Alan, W. (1993). *Grief Avoidance Response Patterns*. Pallicom *USA*, *12*(2).

Alcohol guidelines: Reducing the Health Risks, National Health and Medical Research Council. (2015). *Nhmrc.gov.au*. https://www.nhmrc.gov.au/health-topics/alcohol-guidelines

Amphetamines - Drug Prevention & Alcohol Facts - DrugInfo. (2016). *Druginfo.adf.org.au*, http://www.druginfo.adf.org.au/drug-facts/amphetamines

Are you Sleeping Well? (2001) (1st ed.). Adelaide. Vitalhealth National Pharmacies

Ashfield, J. (1994). *Bereavement Care Referral: Observations for Bereavement Assessment - Adults* (1st ed.). Adelaide: Palliative Care Unit, Royal Adelaide Hospital.

Ashfield, J. (1998). *A Framework and Resources for Bereavement Counselling Practice*. Adelaide: Calvary Hospital.

Ashfield, J. (2003). *Gender, Masculinity and Manhood: Core Concepts for Understanding Men's Issues* (1st ed.). Australia: Ikon International Institute for Healing Arts and Sciences.

Australian Guidelines to Reduce Health Risks from Drinking Alcohol, National Health and Medical Research Council. (2014). *Nhmrc.gov.au*. https://www.nhmrc.gov.au/guidelines-publications/ds10

Bagshaw, D., Chung, D., Couch, M., Lilburn, S., & Wadham, B. (1999). *Reshaping Responses to Domestic Violence*. Adelaide: University of South Australia. http://wesnet.org.au/wp-content/uploads/2012/07/PADV-Reshaping-responses.pdf

Bolton, R. (1986). *People Skills*. New York: Simon & Schuster.

Cannabis - Drug Prevention & Alcohol Facts - DrugInfo. (2003). *Druginfo.adf.org.au*. http://www.druginfo.adf.org.au/drug-facts/cannabis

Causes of Death, Australia - 3303.0, 2014. (2016). *Abs.gov.au*. http://www.abs.gov.au/ausstats/abs@.nsf/mf/3303.0

Conflict Resolution Network. (2003). *Crnhq.org.* http://www.crnhq.org/content.aspx?file=66138|373821

Davies, J. (2003). *A Manual of Mental Health Care in General Practice.* Canberra, A.C.T.: Commonwealth Department of Health and Ageing, Mental Health and Suicide Prevention Branch.

Davis, M., Eshelman, E., & McKay, M. (2008). *The Relaxation & Stress Reduction Workbook.* Oakland, CA: New Harbinger Publications.

Depression in Young People: Publication series, National Health and Medical Research Council. (2014)

Grieflink. (2016). *Palassist.org.au.* http://palassist.org.au/services/grieflink/

Hassan, R. (1995), *Suicide Explained: The Australian Experience,* Melbourne University Press, Carlton South

Ice - Drug Prevention & Alcohol Facts - DrugInfo. (2016). *Druginfo.adf.org.au.* http://www.druginfo.adf.org.au/drug-facts/ice

Insomnia Management. (2000) (1st ed.). Adelaide. Department of Human Services, Environmental Health Branch

Keks, Nicholas A. & Burrows, Graham D. (1998). *Mental Health.* North Sydney, N.S.W Australasian Medical Publishing Company

Misuse of pharmaceuticals - web fact sheet - *Drug Prevention & Alcohol Facts - DrugInfo.* (2016). Druginfo.adf.org.au. http://www.druginfo.adf.org.au/fact-sheets/misuse-of-pharmaceuticals-web-fact-sheet

National Drug Strategy Household Survey 2013 (AIHW). (2016). *Aihw.gov.au* http://www.aihw.gov.au/alcohol-and-other-drugs/ndshs-2013/

National Survey of Mental Health and Wellbeing: Summary of Results - 4326.0, 2007. (2016). *Abs.gov.au.* http://www.abs.gov.au/AUSSTATS/abs@.nsf/DetailsPage/4326.02007?OpenDocument

SAMHSA. (2016). *Samhsa.gov.* http://www.samhsa.gov/

Schut, M. (1999). *The Dual Process Model of Coping with Bereavement: Rationale and Description.* Death Studies, 23(3), 197-224. http://dx.doi.org/10.1080/074811899201046

Scott, A. (1995). Lehrer, Paul M. & Woolfolk, Robert L. (Eds.). (1993*). Principles and Practice of Stress Management* (2nd ed.). New York: Guilford Press, xvi. pp. 621. $65.00. American Journal of Clinical Hypnosis, *37*(3), 80-82. http://dx.doi.org/10.1080/00029157.1995.10403149

Stroebe, M., Stroebe, W., & Hansson, R. (1993). *Handbook of Bereavement.* Cambridge [England]: Cambridge University Press.

Teen Health - Health Topics - Conflict and Negotiation. (2016). *Cyh.com.* http://www.cyh.com/HealthTopics/HealthTopicDetails.aspx?p=243&np=291&id=2183

The Right Mix: Your Health and Alcohol. (2015). https://www.therightmix.gov.au/assets/images/order/pdfs/P00847_Right_Mix_Brochure_2009_2.pdf

Treatment Protocol Project & Andrews, Gavin & Hunt, Caroline & Jarry, Malinda & World Health Organization. Collaborating Centre for Mental Health and Substance

Abuse (issuing body) (2000). *Management of Mental Disorders* (3rd Australian ed). Darlinghurst, N.S.W. World Health Organization Collaborating Centre for Mental Health and Substance Abuse

Walter, T. (1996). *A New Model of Grief: Bereavement and Biography*. Mortality, 1(1), 7-25. http://dx.doi.org/10.1080/713685822

Williams, R. (1997) *Anger Kills*. ABC Radio National Australia transcript 7 April 1997

Wolfelt, D. (1993). *Grief Avoidance and Response Patterns*, Center for Loss and Life Transistion, Colorado, US

Worden, J. (2009). *Grief Counseling and Grief Therapy*. New York, NY: Springer Pub. Co.

Young Adult Health - Health Topics - Anger. (2016). *Cyh.com*. http://www.cyh.com/HealthTopics/HealthTopicDetails.aspx?p=240&np=298&id=2130

NOTES

NOTES

www.ingramcontent.com/pod-product-compliance
Lightning Source LLC
Chambersburg PA
CBHW060502090426
42735CB00011B/2086